WHEN THE LIGHTS GO ON AGAIN

A YOUNG PERSON'S VIEW OF LIFE ON THE HOME FRONT DURING WWII

MARGARET WALTERS WITH MARK WALTERS

authorHOUSE®

AuthorHouse™
1663 Liberty Drive
Bloomington, IN 47403
www.authorhouse.com
Phone: 1-800-839-8640

First published by AuthorHouse 10/6/2010

ISBN: 978-1-4520-8014-7 (sc)
ISBN: 978-1-4520-8015-4 (hc)
ISBN: 978-1-4520-8016-1 (e)

Library of Congress Control Number: 2010914353

Printed in the United States of America

This book is printed on acid-free paper.

A NOTE TO THE READER

The Second World War was a brutal war, even more so than most wars. Millions fought, and some fifty million died, and not just men—women and children also died by the millions in "the old worlds" of Europe and Asia.   Indeed, the Second World War was one of the few wars in which more civilian non-combatants died than did soldiers.

The war impacted societies in ways that were both positive and negative. On the positive side, American society was probably never more unified than during World War II—unified in its determination to defeat fascism and Nazism, and to bring the world back from the brink of a new Dark Age.   Unfortunately, this unity also contributed to a shameful chapter in American history: the internment of thousands of Americans of Japanese ancestry.

The world in which Elaine lived was absorbed by the War.   In telling about this very different world, this book uses the language of that time; not to do so would be to diminish the suffering and sacrifice of the Japanese American population of the West Coast.

We hope that readers will understand that the language of America in the 1940s is not the language of America in the 21st century; like Elaine, America has grown up.

CHAPTER 1

Mid-October, 1945

"Students," announced Miss Worth from her desk on the corner of the stage of the old auditorium, "for social studies today we have a special treat. Arthur Lea is going to tell us about what it was like living in the Philippines under Japanese occupation." There was a rustle of excitement among the other students as Arthur left his seat and walked toward the steps to the stage. Throughout World War II, people had crowded into Fresno, California, where Elaine lived. Now Elaine's school, John Muir Elementary, was so overcrowded that the auditorium had been turned into a classroom for the whole sixth grade—all seventy students.

Arthur was just one of the many new students enrolled since the war ended. But he was far and away the most interesting. He fascinated all the sixth graders. For the boys, it was the fact that Arthur had been *there*, right in the middle of the war that had been so central to their lives for the last four years. For the girls, it was Arthur's mysterious dark eyes and the handsomeness of his features. For Elaine it was something else entirely. Something in the way he acted. He seemed to have confidence, seemed to be in charge of himself. His sister had told everybody he was fifteen. 'Was it true?' Elaine wondered. 'Fifteen years old and still in the sixth grade?' But if Arthur were from the Philippines, it would explain a lot. The Japanese had invaded the Philippines three days after they bombed Pearl Harbor. One by one, the Japanese had captured all of the Philippine Islands. They had occupied them for three and a half years. 'Maybe the Japanese did not let Arthur go to school,' she thought. 'That would explain why he's only in the sixth grade.'

Elaine could hardly wait to hear him tell his story. She often let her mind wander when she was in class, but today her attention was fixed on the front of the room. Elaine watched with growing excitement as Arthur walked up the three steps and out onto the small stage. He smiled. To the

1

sixth grade girls it was a wonderful smile, full of white teeth shining out from a light brown face. He pushed his dark hair back from his forehead, a sign of anxiety Elaine had never seen him display before. He began:

"I was born in a small town in the Philippines." His voice was calm, full of confidence. His accent was pleasing, almost melodic. "I lived with my mother, father, and sister. My father was an important man in the town where we lived. When the Japanese overran our island, there was not much we could do about it. We had no weapons, no army. We had to surrender. My father and many of the other men fled to the mountains to fight the Japanese as freedom fighters. My father's men stole weapons and explosives from the Japanese. Sometimes they came home in the middle of the night, to get food and see their families before they returned to the mountains.

"One night, early in the War, my father asked me to leave with him. He said they needed me to help fight the Japanese."

Elaine thought back over the many stories she had heard during the war—of brave men, women, and even children sacrificing their safety, and sometimes their lives too, in the struggle against the Nazis and Imperial Japan. It had all sounded like such a great adventure!

"I was small," he continued. "My father said his men could put me through a window and I could then open the door for them. I wanted to go with my father and the other men. I hated the Japanese. They did terrible things to us. They had no business in my country. I was proud that I could help fight them.

"So I went to live with my father in the mountains. We would come down from the mountains to blow up bridges, destroy Japanese equipment, and kill as many of them as we could. The Japanese would send patrols after us and we would have to hide. Sometimes we could ambush the patrols.

"One day we came down from the mountains to a house the Japanese were using. One of our lookouts had been watching the house for days. The lookout had come and told us he had seen the Japanese leave in a truck. He said all the Japanese were gone. So we came down to see what trouble we could cause for them while they were gone. We crept up to the house. One of my father's men lifted me up to the window. I cut the glass just like they told me to. I put a piece of hide over the cut glass to protect myself from the sharp edge. I crawled through the window. And in the house …-"

His voice broke.

He paused.

He started again:

"And in the house…"

Again his voice broke.

There was not a sound in the class. Elaine was spellbound; the room was quieter in that moment than at any time she could remember. Arthur looked as if he were seeing something too awful to look at. Everyone saw the horror on his face and the terror in his eyes. No one moved.

Arthur tried one more time,

"And in the house, I saw…."

He stopped, then, and stared off into space. Then, he began to sob. He took a deep breath and tried to begin again. But try as he might, he just couldn't. There, on the small stage, in front of the whole sixth grade, he broke into tears. Miss Worth hurried onto the stage and led him gently to his seat.

The rest of the classroom went totally, dead silent. Arthur's weeping and muffled sobs were the only sounds.

Miss Worth commanded, "Pupils, take out a piece of paper. Write three hundred words about the best birthday you ever had. Be descriptive. Tell when it was, where it was, and what made it special."

Everyone started writing, or at least pretended to write. The room was still perfectly silent, save for the soft sound of Arthur's sobbing.

From her seat in the rear of the classroom, Elaine tried to shut out the sound of the muffled sobs of her classmate. Elaine had always been a good student, one who followed the teacher's instructions. But this time, she couldn't. As hard as she tried, she still couldn't shut out the sound and think about birthdays.

She, like every student in the class, wanted to know what had made Arthur so upset. But she knew that none of them would ever ask him. For four years, Elaine had lived by the rule: never, ever talk about the war with grownups, except, of course, your own parents. And even though Arthur was no grownup, she knew the rule applied to him also.

Elaine just stared at the piece of lined newsprint on her desk. She tried to think about birthdays. All that came into her head were horrific images she had seen in a newsreel last spring about the liberation of a prisoner of war camp in the Philippines. At first she had covered her eyes in horror, but then, when curiosity got the better of her, she had peeked between her fingers at the pictures of the Americans who had been Japanese prisoners of war. Images glared out at her—skeletal men in ragged clothes, staring out of hollow eyes, smiling with toothless mouths, shriveled hands feebly waving at the camera, the first two fingers spread in a "V", for victory. She had been revolted by the sight of these skeletal, sick old men. Even as she had watched, there was a part of her that just couldn't believe it. She knew that most of these soldiers were younger than her father.

Elaine tried to think about birthdays. Sitting in class, staring at the empty paper, made her think of the time she'd asked her mother how anyone could treat fellow human beings the way the prisoners had obviously been treated. Her mother, who believed in the basic goodness of all people, had given an explanation. "The Japanese honor code demands that a soldier fight to the death. They think of military prisoners as dishonorable men, not fit to be treated as human beings. Besides, the best Japanese men were fighting, not guarding prisoners. Those Japanese left on guard duty felt shamefully dishonored because they were not in combat. They took their feelings of shame out on the prisoners." Elaine could barely look at the American strangers she had seen in that newsreel. Had Arthur seen friends, or even relatives, in similar conditions? Tales of torture at the hands of the Japanese had been told all through the war. Had Arthur seen a man he had fought with, or worse yet, a civilian neighbor, with marks of torture on him? Then there were the stories of soldiers collecting body parts from fallen enemies. *What had Arthur seen in that house?* Elaine tried to think of birthdays, but Arthur's sobbing still echoed in her ears.

"Elaine, you need to get to work," Miss Worth scolded. Elaine sighed, picked up her pen, and wrote "Elaine West" at the top of the page. Trying to block out the sound of Arthur's soft sobbing, Elaine began to think about birthdays. What came to her mind was her seventh birthday. It was the one she best remembered, although it was certainly not the best, but rather the worst, birthday she had ever had. Elaine could still remember how confused and hurt she had felt that day, how little she had understood.

On that day, nearly four years ago now, Elaine remembered hearing the news that would change her life and the lives of everyone around her, swiftly and permanently. That day was December 7th, 1941.

CHAPTER 2

December 7, 1941

On that birthday, a much younger Elaine sat in church with her family. She pulled absentmindedly on one of the ringlets in her hair while she looked around the sanctuary. Usually, her hair was only slightly wavy. But last night, Mother had carefully set her hair in rag curlers and then that morning combed the light brown strands into ringlets. This day was special, after all, and Elaine wanted to look the part.

She twisted in her seat and looked around the sanctuary. "Look!" she whispered to her older sister Sara, who was sitting next to her, "There's Andy and Bob." She pointed at two men dressed in Army Air Corps uniforms, sitting side by side on the other side of the church. Bob caught her gaze and gave her a big smile and a slight wave.

Mother reached over the lap of Elaine's younger brother, Billy, and put her hand on Elaine's knee. "Shhh," she signaled with her finger to her lip. Sara nudged Elaine's ribs with her elbow and gave her a look that said, 'don't you *dare* embarrass me, I don't care if it *is* your birthday'. Elaine slumped back in the pew—Mother to the right, Sara to the left. As the middle child, Elaine was sure she got the worst of it.

She continued to look around the sanctuary. There were several other men in uniform in the church, but she didn't know any of them. They were from the Fresno Army Air Base on the edge of town. Sara had said that the airbase was being enlarged to protect the Panama Canal from the Germans. But, as far as Elaine could tell, no one in Fresno really seemed too worried about the Germans. They were far away in Europe. The rest of the world might be at war, but America was at peace. America was safe, protected by its oceans.

She didn't even know either Andy's or Bob's last names. But the last several Sundays, they had eaten dinner at the Wests' home. Father was one of many church members who invited attending servicemen home

5

for dinner after church. The men were lonely, and far from home. Those family visits helped keep up their morale, so Father said.

Rev. Markson began his sermon and Elaine's mind began to wander. Elaine thought of the family birthday celebration that would come after church. She could hardly wait. Her birthday was the one day in the whole year when she could count on being the center of the family's attention. Attention was difficult for her to get. Sara got extra privileges and responsibilities because she was the oldest. Billy was adored for being a boy, and pampered for being the youngest. In so many ways, Elaine felt she was a disappointment from birth, especially to her Father, whose real name was John West. After all, she'd been born in the Great Depression, when her father had been out of work for years. But on her birthday, she knew things would be different. She knew everyone would go out of the way to make her feel really special. Following church, her grandparents, and probably Bob and Andy, would join them for a birthday dinner

The family greatly enjoyed Bob and Andy's Sunday visits. Andy was from a farm in Indiana. He said Elaine reminded him of his sister who was about her age. Billy, Elaine, and Sara all enjoyed playing checkers and pick-up-sticks with him. He gave Billy a handicap of four, Elaine a two, and Sara a one. Sara and he were usually neck and neck, but sometimes Elaine or Billy won. Elaine suspected that, sometimes, Andy and Sara let one of them win. Win or lose, when they played together there was always a lot of laughing. Bob was a little older than Andy. He had left a wife and baby at home in Akron, Ohio. He and Father both enjoyed fishing. They always seemed to have a lot to talk about.

As Rev. Markson droned on, Elaine thought about the birthday party Mother had held for her and her friends the day before. They had played games, eaten cake and ice cream, and then Elaine had opened her presents. Elaine thought the best present was the beautiful set of jacks with a red ball in their own little leather bag. Jacks were what the girls played at school during recess, while the boys played marbles. The jacks were a gift from Rae Dean.

Rae Dean lived down the street. She and Elaine often played at each other's houses. They also quarreled a lot, and it was usually because each of them wanted to be the boss. The week before, Elaine had attended Rae Dean's birthday party. That party had been very crowded, as Rae Dean's house was so small. Rae Dean's father worked at a place called Pearl Harbor. All Elaine knew about Pearl Harbor was that it was very far away.

It was so far away that Rae Dean's father had mailed her birthday present in July, just to be sure that the ship got it there in time.

At the party, Rae Dean's wealthy grandmother had given Rae Dean a Storybook Doll. Rae Dean collected Storybook Dolls. She had Snow White, Little Red Riding Hood, Cinderella, and half a dozen more. This doll, with its long, softly curling amber hair, thickly lashed closed eyes, pink cheeks, and slightly smiling mouth had to be Sleeping Beauty. Rae Dean's grandmother had also said that she was giving Rae Dean bonds. Rae Dean did not seem to care about the bonds, but her mother had been very excited. The bonds were not at the party. Elaine thought Rae Dean had been given bombs. She wasn't quite sure what bombs were, but she didn't think they were something you normally gave as a gift. She wondered where the bombs were, and what they looked like. Rae Dean's mother had thought that the bombs—or bonds, or whatever they were—were a wonderful gift, but Rae Dean had liked the Storybook Doll of Sleeping Beauty much better.

But today was Elaine's birthday, not Rae Dean's. As soon as church was over she'd be the center of attention, and she couldn't wait. Elaine wondered how long it would be. And then she realized that it was completely silent in the church. Something was happening. Something important. She realized for the first time that Rev. Markson had suddenly stopped talking. Now, in a different tone of voice he made an announcement. Elaine heard a gasp from the entire congregation. Everyone's attention was focused on the man in the pulpit. In his hands was a piece of paper.

"I repeat," he said, "the Japanese have attacked Pearl Harbor. They have dropped bombs on the port and on our ships. There is much damage. There are casualties. This is all that was on the radio. Maybe we'll know more later. I suggest that we close this service with a prayer so we can go to our homes and listen to the radio."

Elaine was sure she had misunderstood. Never before had a church service ended early! But, sure enough, everyone was bowing their heads as Rev. Markson led a short prayer. Usually, when led in prayer, the people in the congregation were restless, but today there was no sound except the voice of Reverend Markson. People looked like they were really praying. Now the organ was playing and people were excitedly talking to one another as they left their pews and walked from the church.

Out in the parking lot, Bob and Andy were standing at the center of a group of people, talking. Andy looked worried and upset, while Bob reminded Elaine of the way Father always looked before he started a difficult job. The other uniformed airmen also seemed to be surrounded by groups of people. No one looked happy.

Elaine was confused. Pearl Harbor was where Rae Dean's father was. Bombs were what Rae Dean had gotten from her rich grandparents for her birthday. The whole thing made no sense. Elaine put it from her mind.

She was pleased to be out of church so early. "It's my birthday!" she announced to Reverend Markson as she passed him. She paused then, and waited patiently for the expected pat on the head. But he seemed not to hear her. He was earnestly talking with a group of church members. Elaine waited for a gap in the conversation and tugged on his coat. "Today is my birthday!" she repeated.

"That's nice," He barely glanced in her direction before resuming his conversation.

"Come on, Elaine!" Sara grabbed her arm and pulled her toward the parking lot. "Don't make a pest of yourself! Can't you tell everyone is upset?"

"What's going on?" asked Elaine

Before Sara could answer, Mother called. "Come on girls! We need to get going! Go get into Grandpa's car."

"Where's our car?" asked Elaine.

"Your father is using it to take Bob and Andy back to the base."

"But, aren't they coming to my birthday dinner!?!" Elaine had had enough. She had suffered about all the disappointment she could take.

"No, dear. They need to get back to the base. They may be needed."

"But it's my *birthday!*"

"I know, dear, and I'm sorry! Please, don't make a fuss!"

Elaine knew that if even Mother was ignoring her birthday, there must be a good reason. Still, it just wasn't fair—it was her *birthday*, for goodness' sake. Didn't anybody understand that? She sat in the back seat of her grandparent's 1936 Plymouth and tried to figure out why the dropping of bombs, whatever they were, on Pearl Harbor, wherever that was, was more important than her birthday. No one spoke and everyone strained to hear the car radio. When Elaine tried to ask questions, Sara shushed her. "Just be quiet, Elaine!" she said, "Everyone wants to hear the radio!"

Elaine slumped down in her seat, folded her arms and made a sour face. She was not happy.

Once they arrived home, Mother turned on the radio in the living room. Father arrived home shortly later, visibly upset. While Mother and Sara put the dinner on the table, Father and Grandpa talked of battleships, carriers, zeros, and allies. From the name Elaine had some idea of what battleships must be, but carriers, allies, and zeros? The whole thing made no sense. No one would answer Elaine's questions—not even Mother, who usually liked to explain things. When they sat down to eat, Grandpa said a long and serious prayer, which had little to do with the food they were going to eat. Then Mother said, "Let's all remember today is Elaine's birthday. Let's make it a good day for her." But only Billy seemed to hear.

The day continued to be disappointing. Although Mother served Elaine's favorite foods, and insisted that everyone sing "Happy Birthday" when she brought in the birthday cake, the mood at the dinner table was far from festive. Father had turned the radio up so loud that Elaine could hear it from the other room. And if anybody tried to talk, Father put his finger in front of his mouth and said 'shush'. Mother went through the motions of a birthday celebration. She knew how important it was to Elaine. But it was clear that even Mother was upset. She, too, seemed distracted by the radio. Grandmother, who hated President Roosevelt, kept muttering that the Japanese attack was somehow Roosevelt's fault. Only Sara and Billy paid much attention while Elaine opened her presents.

Once dinner was over Sara tried with all her patience to explain to Elaine what had happened. "Japanese planes flew off of a ship and dropped bombs on a Navy base in Hawaii named Pearl Harbor. It was a big surprise."

"But Rae Dean got bombs for her birthday." Elaine was still puzzled. "That's what her grandmother said."

"That's not what her grandmother said. You just don't understand," said Sara. "Rae Dean did not get *bombs* for her birthday, she got *bonds*. Bombs explode when they hit something. They kill people. These bombs sank ships and killed lots of people."

Sara was right. Elaine didn't understand it all. Nothing in her experience gave her the background to understand. Billy, at four years old, understood even less. But even he knew something terrible had happened.

That night, Elaine had trouble sleeping. The radio was still on in the living room, and when Elaine snuck to the door, she saw Mother and Father still sitting next to it. Father was smoking his old oak pipe, and listening. Mother, who usually read, was just staring out the window, stone faced.

Elaine didn't know what to make of any of it. And for the first time since she could remember, she started to feel very frightened.

"Elaine!" it was Sara's voice, just behind her, "we're all scared; Father, Mother, Billy, and I, too. But there's nothing we can do about it now. Come get some sleep."

Elaine turned, and watched the sliver of light disappear as she closed the door.

CHAPTER 3

Mid-December, 1941

The children had always loved the lights downtown. It was sort of a custom, when out at night, for Father to drive up and down Fulton, the main street, very, very slowly. While Mother and Sara studied the brightly lit display windows of the larger stores, Elaine and Billy enjoyed the brightly colored neon lights. A large number of these neon signs made pictures—some even blinked, tricking the eye into seeing movement. Billy's favorites were the red fire truck, blue car, and yellow tractor that took turns running across the wall above the window of the toy store. Elaine's favorite was the sign in front of the fur store. On it, a red fox ran up the sign and disappeared, only to magically reappear at the bottom.

"Dragging the Main", as this custom was called, was especially nice at Christmastime, when every streetlight pole was decorated with tinsel and lights and the display windows had special scenes in them. As far back as Elaine could remember, those lights had signaled to her that Christmas was near.

But this year there were no lights. Dark were the Christmas lights, the neon signs, the shop window lights, even the light on the courthouse dome. Off, too, were the lights in the rest of the city, the streetlights, the Christmas decorations, even the neighborhood porch lights. The top of the Tower Theater, just two blocks from the Wests' home, went dark. From their porch, they had been able to see the last few feet of its elongated, three-sided tower with the starburst on top, dazzling over the dark shapes of the neighbor's houses. Before Pearl Harbor, the tower had been lighted with every color of the rainbow, each blinking in turn, while the starburst was a golden orb with rays of differing lengths flashing into the night. But now it was dark. Only the traffic lights remained, and they had been fitted with shades so their light, feeble as it was, could not be seen from the air. The whole city was hiding in the dark. The darkness frightened Elaine. The adults thought the Japanese might bomb Fresno, just like they'd bombed Pearl Harbor.

The day after her disappointing birthday, Elaine had resolved to listen to the radio whenever it was on. She was determined not to be caught off-guard again, and to understand what was going on, so she wouldn't have to ask so many questions. This is what she had heard: On December 10th, the Japanese Army had invaded the American-held Territory of the Philippines. But, aside from reports of the invasion, no news was coming out of the Pacific.

In Fresno, even grownups like Father seemed to be very afraid. Would California be next? Elaine did not understand how the war had managed to leap the ocean and threaten her. Was Fresno in real danger of being bombed? Elaine had begun to look at the newspapers and news magazines, too. The pictures on the covers had told her what bombs could do.

Whenever she got the chance, Elaine would ask Mother questions about what she had seen and heard. Elaine tried not to ask too many questions around Father or Sara, because they were always annoyed by it. For questions, Mother was much better.

Early one evening, Elaine was in the kitchen with Mother, helping her prepare dinner. Usually, this was Sara's job, but today was Friday and Sara was staying late at school for some reason. As Mother rolled dough for biscuits, Elaine asked: "Do you think we'll be bombed? Here in Fresno"

"Probably not," Mother replied, "but maybe. Either way, we should be as prepared as possible."

"But why? Fresno's not a naval base."

"No, but it's an airbase, a railroad hub, and an electrical power center. Besides, airplanes have to drop their bombs somewhere before they can fly back to their carriers. If they can't find San Francisco, Oakland, or Alameda because of the fog, then Fresno will be their target."

"Can't we keep the carriers away?"

"We have no navy left, Elaine. Not in that Pacific, anyway. Our battleships were sunk or badly damaged at Pearl Harbor. We simply aren't ready for war."

"Why not?

Mother sighed. "I don't know." Then, she stopped rolling, and turned to look at Elaine. "But you have nothing to worry about. Father and I will keep you safe, whatever happens."

Elaine had never seen Mother quite like this. Something was off, but Elaine couldn't figure out just what.

"Here, Elaine," Mother said, and handed her the dough and a biscuit cutter. "Cut the biscuits for me. It would be a big help."

Elaine took the dough and the cutter, and started in.

The next day was Saturday. Sara, Billy, and Elaine drove with Mother to run an errand. Next to the office where Mother had business was an office with a long line of men outside of it.

"I wonder what those men are all lined up for?" whispered Elaine.

"Look at the signs," said Sara.

On the window was a brightly colored poster, made to catch the eye. From the poster's background of palm trees and blue water a plane swooped out toward the viewer. Each silver wing was marked with a bright red circle. Elaine knew from the pictures she'd seen in the magazines that the circle was the symbol of Japan. Beneath and behind the plane, black smoke billowed from a gray ship already sprouting bright red-orange flames. Towering over the blazing deck, the ship's riggings narrowed to a single thin metal pole from which the red, white, and blue of the American flag snapped proudly in the wind. "Remember Pearl Harbor!" screamed out in bold letters across the bottom. On a stand by the door was a poster of Uncle Sam. He wore a blue coat and top hat, and pointed his finger straight at the viewer. Under this image bold letters announced: "I Want You" and underneath, in smaller print: "to Join the Army."

"They all want to join the Army?" asked Elaine.

"Of course," replied Sara, "everybody's joining up."

Elaine studied the line. The men were all different sizes—some dressed in suits, some in work clothes, some looked like tramps or hobos and some like students. Elaine even saw some who looked East Asian.

"Are some of those men Japanese?" Elaine looked closer, "or Chinese?"

"You just don't understand," said Sara. Like most Californians, she couldn't tell the difference between the two groups, and Fresno had a very large population of both.

When Mother came back they asked her. "Are those men in the line Japanese, or Chinese?"

"I don't know," Mother answered. "They could be Japanese."

"But we're fighting Japan." said Elaine.

"That doesn't mean that the young Japanese who were born here wouldn't fight for their country. America, that is. Those boys have probably never even seen Japan," said Mother.

They rode home. The radio played a new song, "Praise the Lord and Pass the Ammunition", in between Christmas carols. It seemed that everyone wanted to fight. The children knew Father had tried to enlist in the Army Engineering Corps, but he had been turned down because of his age and general health. But Father still wanted to help out, so he volunteered for the Civilian Defense Corps. He was assigned various duties, all having to do with keeping civilians in Fresno safe. He was responsible for the safety of his block. His first duty was to ensure that each household on the block stored emergency water and food, and that each house and business had a bucket of sand and a shovel handy for fighting fires in case the block was bombed. Elaine remembered what Mother had said, about her and Father keeping them all safe, and that made her feel a little better.

Rae Dean, on the other hand, had not even heard from her father, and she was really upset. He had been working for a construction company in Honolulu. The report on the radio said that few civilians were injured or killed by the attack on Pearl Harbor, but he might be one of those few. Days passed, and weeks, and still no word came. The only telegrams coming from Hawaii were those listing the dead military personnel. There was no telephone service, and radio communication was not allowed. Like so many others who had relatives at Pearl Harbor, Rae Dean's family could only wait and hope.

As they walked home from school one day the next week, Elaine, Sara, and Rae Dean all compared their air raid drill experiences. The air raid drills had started just a week after the attack on Pearl Harbor, and they had completely transformed school.

Each drill went something like this: in each downstairs classroom, the students were lined up and marched into the cloakroom. Every classroom but the kindergarten had a cloakroom, which was a long, narrow room where students hung their coats on hooks along the wall and left their lunchboxes. In the past, the cloakroom had been the place to which misbehaving students were sent, shut away for who knew how long; now, it was to be the refuge for the students if the Japanese bombers came. During air-raid drills, no talking was allowed in the cloakroom, but whispering was overlooked. It was also a place to share secrets and make plans for recess.

Once in the cloakroom, the students sat with their back against the wall and their legs crossed in front of them. Absolutely no talking was allowed. The students just sat there with their heads down and their hands clasped behind their necks. They sat there for what seemed like hours.

But though that had been Elaine's experience, Sara told a different story: "I had to line up like for a fire drill and go downstairs to the lunchroom. There, our class had to sit under the tables we are assigned to eat lunch at. We, too, had to protect our neck and head."

"Where were the benches?" asked Elaine.

"On top of the tables."

"Bombs can't go through lunch tables?" Rae Dean asked.

"Of course they can," said Sara. "The tables are to protect us from flying glass. Our teacher said bombs often break windows for blocks and we were much more likely to be hit by glass than by bombs."

"That must be why we go to the cloakroom," said Elaine, "it only has one window, and it's very small and very high up. Plus, it's been covered with a wire mesh. I guess that's to catch any falling glass."

"I thought fire drills were the boringest things," said Rae Dean, "but I musta been wrong 'cus air raid drills are even boringer."

Christmas came just eighteen days after Pearl Harbor. But so much had changed in those two and a half weeks. Despite their fear, people were determined to celebrate. The decorations were already in place. The streetlights downtown were hung with red bells, silver tinsel, and colored lights. So what if they weren't lighted? The shops were full of things to buy. People had money to spend.

Every year, The Wests looked forward to a drive though Christmas Tree Lane. Christmas Tree Lane had started when one family decorated the evergreen trees in front of their house with lights as a memorial to their son, who had been killed in the Great War. Their neighbors followed their lead and decorated their own trees. Soon the neighborhood association, in honor of all American dead in the Great War, had planted evergreens along both sides of the street for over a mile.

Now, some twenty years later, the trees were huge. The neighborhood association still put lights on the trees every year. Many homeowners added lighted decorations on the lawns and rooftops of their large, beautiful houses. At Christmastime, traffic was one way and very, very slow. Father called it "stop and go." Everyone drove the lane with the windows rolled down to hear the caroling and to call to friends in neighboring cars. Although they always wore their warmest clothes and wrapped up in a wool blanket, the children were still half frozen by the time they got through the lane and rolled up the car windows again. Once home, Mother would make them all cocoa. They loved warming up by sipping hot chocolate in front of a roaring fire in the fireplace. It was one of the things Sara and Elaine liked most about Christmas. But that year, although most of the decorations were already up, Christmas Tree Lane was closed.

There was one other difference in the Wests' Christmas celebration that year. For the first time since Elaine could remember, they had a complete stranger at Christmas dinner. Bob and Andy, who had shared many Sundays with them, had shipped out to the war shortly before Christmas. But new troops were pouring through Fresno almost daily, and Father and Mother hated the thought of young men miles from home at Christmas. So while the women (that is, Grandmother, Mother, Sara, and Elaine) prepared the dinner, Grandpa, Father, and Billy went downtown, and came back with a very homesick marine. His name was Johnny. He was a farm boy from Lockridge, Iowa, who had joined the Marines just months before Pearl Harbor. He had a three day pass, and was due to ship out to the Pacific right after Christmas. Three days was not enough time to go home to Iowa for Christmas, but it was enough time to get away from the ocean at San Diego and into the farming country around Fresno, so Johnny had hopped the train.

Usually, Father and Grandfather did most of the talking at dinner, but this time they sat, almost silently, and just listened as Johnny talked about his parents, and his little brother and sister. He talked of last year's Christmas dinner on the farm in Iowa. He talked about fishing with his friends, and of how he missed his dog. Nobody talked about the war. Mother had planned ahead and wrapped Christmas gifts for him—just some shaving cream, a fancy package of dried fruit, and a small wind-up toy for laughs. After dinner, while Sara and Elaine helped their mother with the dishes, Daddy, Johnny, and Billy went outside to watch Billy ride his new scooter. When they came inside again, Johnny played "go fish" with Sara and Elaine. Toward evening, everyone gathered around the piano, and while Mother played everybody sang Christmas carols. Before Father took Johnny back downtown, Mother set out a cold supper with a hot fruit cobbler for dessert.

After he left, Mother gathered the children together. "I'm proud of the way you let him do the talking and seemed interested in what he had to say.

Entertaining a lonely service man on a special holiday is very important, and I'm so proud of each of you." She handed them each a piece of candy. But before she let them go, she said one more thing:

"Nobody knows how long this war is going to last. But I need each of you to promise me one thing. We'll probably have more guests like Johnny in the future. And, when we do, each of you is never, ever to ask him questions about where he's going, or bring up the war. Okay?"

Elaine, Sara and Billy all nodded. Then Mother let them go and prepare for bed. Elaine's candy was a lemon drop—her favorite.

In bed that night Elaine asked, "Will we ever see Johnny again?"

"I doubt it," said Sara. "He's on his way to the front."

"What's the front?" asked Elaine.

"It's wherever the fighting is. Right now, it's in the Philippines," answered Sara

"We're winning, though, aren't we?"

"No." Sara responded, "We're not."

Elaine was stunned. That made no sense to her—she had looked at the map in school, and Japan was tiny compared to America. How could we possibly lose?

"We will win though, won't we?"

"Oh yes!" said Sara. "We won't quit 'til we do!"

CHAPTER 4

Christmas, 1941

Even though the lights were off all over town, and Christmas Tree Lane was shut down, that Christmas was still a lot of fun. Elaine was extra excited when she opened her present on Christmas morning and found a new toy doctor's kit. She put on the white coat and fastened the round mirror, like the ones real doctors wear, around her forehead. She wanted to be a doctor when she grew up. Not a nurse, a doctor. Some kids said girls couldn't be doctors, but she knew they could. Her church had sent money to a medical clinic in China, and there had been a woman missionary doctor there. But when Elaine was very young, Japan overran China, and the woman doctor was forced to leave. No one knew what had happened to the clinic. The woman doctor was now going around talking in churches, which is how Elaine knew all of this in the first place.

After they had all unwrapped their presents, Elaine, Sara, and Billy headed out into the yard to play with them. Supposedly, most places had snow at Christmastime, but Elaine had never seen any, except on some of the mountains outside of town. The date might be December 25th, but it was sunny in Fresno, and the thermometer on their front porch read 65 degrees.

Elaine took a tongue depressor out of the little black bag and headed toward where Billy was playing in the dirt. She tried to get Billy to sit still while she looked down his throat, but Billy was too busy to be a good patient. He was running his new cars and trucks on the maze of roads he had constructed in the dirt. So, Elaine hunted up Sara. She was on the steps in front of the house, putting on her new ball bearing roller skates. Sara was in fourth grade and could master things that Elaine just couldn't seem to, like roller-skating on the sidewalk without being thrown by the cracks. Sara paused long enough to let her sister look down her throat and listen to her heart with the toy stethoscope. Sara was usually kind to

Elaine. Their mother insisted that the children treat everyone, including family members, the way they wanted to be treated.

"Your heart sounds all bumpy." Elaine couldn't hear anything through the stethoscope, but she pretended she could. Elaine was good at pretending. "Here. You need a pill." Elaine offered Sara a little, round tablet from a bottle of blue pills.

"Thanks." Sara popped the pill in her mouth, and chewed. "Boy! That pill tastes better than any medicine I've ever had. Don't you think I need another one?"

"No, I don't want to run out"

"You know they're just candy. You could always replace them with red-hots." And that ruined it. Sara was a realist who, unlike Elaine, didn't really like to pretend. Still, she would sometimes humor her younger sister, to a point. "I want to skate now, but I promise to come to you if I fall and hurt myself. Now go away and don't bother me."

Elaine put her instruments and pills back into her black bag and went into the kitchen to find Mother.

"Mother, can I go to Rae Dean's?"

.   "It's *may* I go," Mother corrected. Mother had taught school before she married, and correct English usage was important to her. "Why not phone her and ask her to come over here instead?" Mother always preferred that the children play at her house. She liked children, and enjoyed hearing them play.

Elaine placed the call and Rae Dean arrived shortly thereafter. She carried a brand new Story-Book Doll still in its box. "See, isn't she beautiful! She's Rose Red. Even her hair is red. I just love to look at her." Rae Dean held out the box for Elaine's admiration.

"How was your Christmas?" Mother asked, as she helped Rae Dean out of her coat.

"It was alright. I got this doll from my dad, but my mom said it was mailed last summer. It takes so long to get mail from Hawaii. We haven't heard from Dad since Pearl Harbor. Mom tried to send a telegram to him to wish him a merry Christmas, but she couldn't, 'cus the War Department said that the telegraph lines were full, an' that you needed special permission to use 'em. I wish we knew if he was all right now that there's a war. We don't even know if he was at Pearl Harbor when the attack came, 'cus sometimes he worked on other islands an' we don't know nuffin' like if he was bombed, an' if he was hurt, an' if he's still in Pearl Harbor, an' what's he doing."

Rae Dean always talked like that—letting one thing spill into another and another. 'And nobody shushes her,' Elaine thought.

"He is probably fine." said Mother. "The radio said very few civilians were hurt. You'll hear in time. No news is good news." It was clear that Rae Dean's Christmas had been damaged by the worry over her father. Elaine thought maybe she could help. "Here," she said, donning her stethoscope, "let me check your heart."

"Okay," Rae Dean replied. Elaine listened, and this time she heard something but she wasn't sure what. "Your heart sounds all bumpy," she said, "I think you need a pill."

CHAPTER 5

January, 1942

The first Wednesday morning after New Year's, Father left before the children were even out of bed. It seemed strange to them to have breakfast without him, and stranger still that after school that evening he wasn't at the dinner table. Finally, at seven-thirty that night, he came home and Mother heated up the leftovers. The whole family routine was out of order. For two years, Father had worked for Fresno County in the Engineering Department, surveying for roads, bridges, and irrigation canals. But, right after New Years, the Army requisitioned him, along with most of the County Engineering Department's men and equipment. The Army had the right to requisition or take whatever it needed, including people, so now Father was working for the Army whether he wanted to or not. He worked twelve hours a day, and Saturdays too—the Army was in a hurry. They were building a new Army Air Corps base just outside of Fresno, and needed the surveying for the runways done months ago, but since that was now impossible, the Army would have to settle for it being done very quickly.

Even the children knew, from the radio and the way the adults talked, that the war in the Pacific was not going well. American forces seemed to be losing everywhere. To make matters worse, Germany and Italy had declared war against the United States on December eighth, so now there were two war fronts—one in the Pacific, and the other in the Atlantic. From the news on the radio it seemed like most of the country was more concerned about the war in the Atlantic, against Germany and Italy. But for Elaine the war in the Atlantic, Europe, and North Africa was always the *other* war. She had never seen the Atlantic Ocean, Europe, or Africa. She had spent part of every summer playing in the water of the Pacific Ocean. It was the war in the Pacific, against the Japanese, that threatened her. Bob and Andy and the other soldiers who had eaten at her dining room table were the only soldiers she knew, and they were all fighting or preparing to fight in the Pacific. For Elaine, the war in Europe was just background noise.

One morning in mid-January, when it was almost time for school, the doorbell rang. It was Rae Dean and she was early. The Wests' house was on her way to school, so she always dropped by in the morning so that she, Elaine, and Sara could all walk to school together.

"Hi, Rae Dean," Mother said. "How are you?"

"Okay, but we still haven't heard from my dad" Rae Dean needed to talk to an adult, and many times she would burst into tears when she told one what was worrying her. That's why she often came to Mother.

"I've heard that there is no civilian mail coming from Hawaii," Mother responded. "He's probably writing, the mail just isn't getting here. No news is most likely good news. I'll bet he's fine. Would you like a cookie to eat on your way to school?' Mother believed that all problems could be helped with food.

Cookies in hand, the children started off for school. As soon as they crossed, the street they met up with Tommy. Tommy, like Rae Dean and Elaine, was in the second grade. He and Elaine were in the same class, whereas Rae Dean was in another. He lived across the street and was the only person Elaine knew who did not like candy.

"Remember, we have to keep our eyes open for 'cendiary devices," said Tommy.

"What's a 'cendiary device?" asked Rae Dean.

"It's sort of a bomb that doesn't explode when it hits. It explodes later, to set fires." Sara explained. "Didn't your teacher tell you to look for them?"

"No, we had a substitute all last week."

"Well, we're supposed to look for them, and if we find one tell a grownup," Tommy continued.

"Whadda they look like?" Rae Dean wanted to help.

"Nobody knows. But the teacher said that they probably don't look like bombs." Tommy shrugged.

"But how can we look for somethin' if we don' know what it looks like?" They had all been puzzling over that, but it was Rae Dean who finally asked the question. And, naturally, it was Sara who finally answered it.

"Just keep your eyes open for anything strange and report it. And don't touch it, it might explode." Sara told it as the teacher had.

"But where would they come from? I mean, how would they get here?" Rae Dean was not going to let the subject drop.

"Airplanes drop them. A plane could fly over almost any time, and nobody would notice because there are lots of planes over our heads all the time, what with the Army Airmen practicing." Sara continued to explain. "Besides, they'd probably do it at night."

Rae Dean shook her head. "I still don' see how we can find 'cendiary devices if we don' know what they look like."

At school that day, during the morning recess, Elaine's class was playing one of its favorite games. The game had no name and no rules and consisted mainly of boys chasing girls across the playfield and into the girls' bathroom. Jimmy Wong, a boy in her class, was chasing Elaine. She was getting far ahead when she heard somebody yell, "There he is! Get him." When Elaine turned around, Jimmy was gone. Then she saw that a bunch of older boys had Jimmy pinned up against the brick wall of the boys' room. "You dirty Jap!" someone yelled. "We're gonna teach you a lesson, Nip."

"But I'm not a Jap!" Jimmy wailed, "I'm …"

Before he could finish his sentence, one of the boys punched him in the stomach, and Jimmy doubled over and fell into the dirt.

Elaine was paralyzed. She didn't know what to do. Some of the other second-graders had gathered and they were screaming at the older boys.

"Stop! Stop! Leave him alone! He's Chinese." The older boys didn't seem to hear. They just kept calling Jimmy names and kicking dirt into his face. Whenever he tried to get up one of the boys moved in and punched him again.

The shrill sound of a whistle made Elaine jump. The older boys straightened up; the second-graders just stood there. Miss Huff, a teacher, hurried over. By the time she got there, the older boys were gone and Jimmy lay in a heap, sobbing.

"What's going on?" Miss Huff demanded.

Before anyone could answer, the bell rang and the children all ran to line up.

Back in the classroom, Elaine sat next to Jimmy at a table they shared with two other students. "Are you hurt?" she asked him.

"Not really, I guess." His face was still dirty save for the streaks that ran from his eyes to his chin, and Elaine knew he was lying about not being hurt. "I'm just tired of people looking at me and thinking I'm Japanese. My uncle got beat up by a bunch a men who thought he was a Jap, an' nobody even stepped in to help him. Even when the police finally got there they just stood and watched. Now everyone in my family is afraid to go anywhere, an' I'm not even safe at school!"

Later that day, a messenger came from the office and handed a note to the teacher. She read it to herself and then to the whole class. "Students," she said, "fighting is not allowed at school for any reason. Students who start fights or pick on smaller kids will be given detention. Further, there are no Japanese students in our school. The Chinese are our friends and allies. China was fighting Japan long before Pearl Harbor." Evidently, the principal had heard about what had happened at recess.

When Elaine got home from school, Mother was ironing, as she usually did on Tuesdays. Elaine loved ironing day. Ironing pinned Mother to one place, but didn't take much of her attention. It was the best time for a talk.

"Mother," Elaine said, "an awful thing happened at recess today." Elaine went on to tell her about the thing that had happened with Jimmy and the older boys.

When Elaine finished, Mother paused, iron in hand, and looked at her. "And Elaine, would it have been okay to beat Jimmy up if he'd been Japanese?" Elaine knew this was no ordinary question. Something in Mother's look said, 'Think before you answer'.

"No." Elaine shook her head. "Kids can't be blamed for what grownups do."

Mother smiled and nodded. "And what could you have done to help Jimmy?"

"I guess I could have run for the teacher," Elaine had thought of this shortly after recess, and was a bit ashamed that she hadn't thought of it in time to help Jimmy.

"Well, next time you'll know what to do." Mother reassured her.

Elaine then told Mother about what had happened to Jimmy's uncle.

Again her mother paused and looked at her. "And if the man who was beaten up had been Japanese, would that have been okay?"

Elaine thought about that even longer. "Not,",she said, "if he'd lived here a long time."

"And if he'd lived here a short time?" Mother was not going to let Elaine off the hook easily.

"Well, I guess that would depend on whether or not he had anything to do with Pearl Harbor."

"Exactly," Mother nodded, "and who decides that?

Elaine didn't answer right away, so Mother prodded. "Men in the street?"

"No," Elaine shook her head.

"So if not men in the street, then who?" asked Mother. It was a question for which Elaine had no answer.

Elaine was playing jacks in her favorite corner of the living room when Father came home from work. Elaine liked to play jacks in that corner, because the oval rug didn't reach into it very far. It left a large space of hardwood floor that gave the jacks ball a perfect bounce. She was not very good at jacks, but practice would make her better.

Usually, when Father came home from work he said hello to Mother and then sat in his favorite chair and started reading the newspaper. Mother would find a break from her work in the kitchen and bring him a glass of water. But this evening he strode straight into the kitchen. Elaine stopped playing and moved closer to the kitchen so she could hear the conversation.

"Alice, this morning Frank—you know Frank, the one with the ranch on the edge of town—well, he told me that his neighbor, a Japanese farmer, had the branches broken off all his fruit trees last night. The farmer saw the men who did it. He thought it was some of the same men who bought apricots and peaches from him just last summer. He called the sheriff on them, but nobody came."

"I know, John," Mother said, "I feel so bad about what's happening to the Japanese people around Fresno. Most of them are just small farmers. Like that family that raises strawberries out by where your parents live. Why, I heard in the store today that people are trampling the crops of Japanese farmers like them. And my goodness... you should talk to Elaine about what happened at her school today..."

"People are angry, and who knows what side the Japanese around here are on?" said Father.

"But shouldn't they be given the benefit of the doubt, John? We have laws, courts…"

"Spies could do a lot of damage while the police look for proof."

"I don't know," sighed Mother, "it reminds me too much of what people did to the Germans in the last war. Why, I went to school with German kids and they saluted the flag like everybody else. But the windows in their houses were smashed anyway. Their families were forced out of business and had to leave town. People felt bad about it later, and said they'd never let that kind of thing happen again. But now the Japanese are getting it worse than the Germans did then." Mother's voice lowered, but Elaine could still make out what she said, "I can't help but wonder if it isn't just because they don't look like the rest of us."

"More likely it's because the attack was so sneaky," argued Father. "I'm not sure I can trust them, Alice, and I'm not alone here. Most people I talk to agree with me."

Elaine heard Father returning to the living room, so she hurried to her jacks corner and pretended she'd been there all along. But she was troubled. She planned to ask Mother about it all later.

CHAPTER 6

January, 1942

The huge central valley of California was rich farmland. The climate was excellent for growing fruit, grapes, olives, and nuts. Fresno was its major city, the farming capitol of California. It was also a railroad hub. From there, trains went north, south, east, and even west to the Port of Oakland on San Francisco Bay. One of the trains that left from Fresno daily in the summertime was the Pacific Fruit Express. This special train carried the fruit and produce grown in the area to markets far to the east. Fresh fruit was carried in insulated icebox cars that were really just giant ice chests. There were holes in the bottom of the cars so the water from the melted ice could escape. Near the edge of the yards, the icehouse made ice in bathtub-sized blocks that were used to ice the cars. Once the cars were loaded with fruit and ice, the Pacific Fruit Express left the yards, pulled by two engines, each followed by a tender car holding the water and coal that were needed to keep the steam engine going. The express steamed across the valley at ninety miles an hour, an almost unheard of speed. It was an exciting sight. The Pacific Fruit Express was the fastest thing on wheels. At the foothills of the Sierra Nevada Mountains, engineers added two more engines behind the caboose to push the train up the steep mountain passes. It wound up the mountains like a snake with a bellyache, struggling through tunnels that had been dug by Chinese laborers three generations before. The hiss of steam and the chugging of the engines competed with the pounding of the wheels on the track as the train inched up the steep grade. Once over the pass, squealing air brakes struggled to keep the train from hurtling off the track, as the weight of the cars forced the front engines down the hill.

Once the train was over the mountains, the extra engines left. The Great Plains spread out in front of the train. There was nothing but farms, small towns, and open sky for hundreds of miles. Across the Great Plains,

The Pacific Fruit Express sped down the tracks so fast that the cars on the highway beside the tracks seemed to be standing still. All other trains, even passenger trains which usually had the right of way, stood still on a siding when The Pacific Fruit Express roared by.

If the weather was not too hot, and the train stopped only to change crews and pick up water and coal, the Pacific Fruit Express would get its peaches, plums, apricots, nectarines, cherries, grapes and so on to the people in the East before the ice melted and the fruit spoiled. It could reach Chicago in three days and New York in four.

John Wests' parents, Elaine's grandparents, lived just outside of Fresno. Grandpa West worked for the Southern Pacific Railroad, and often told Elaine stories about what it was like. They lived in the comfortable house that came with Grandpa's railroad job. It was painted the same ugly orange-brown color used on boxcars, probably with the same paint. There was a large yard that included olive trees, a garden area, and even a chicken coop, with chickens.

The younger Wests visited them often. Elaine had never really gotten along with her grandmother. Grandmother West always seemed to find fault with her. Elaine was un-ladylike. She was too talkative. She tracked in dirt. If Elaine so much as handled anything, her grandmother scolded her for not putting it back in the right place. Elaine's grandmother was always telling her she should be more like Sara. Sara and grandmother enjoyed each other's company. They would talk and stitch together for hours. Grandmother West did beautiful needlework. She was passing her expertise on to Sara. She had given up on Elaine, who seemed to be all thumbs and never finished what she started. Grandmother no longer even offered to show Elaine how to do anything. She really seemed to prefer that Elaine not even be around. That was fine with Elaine, who usually wanted to be outside anyway.

Grandpa West, too, seemed to prefer being outside. He was so different from his wife that it was hard to imagine them living together. Grandpa loved people, but he especially loved children—the noisier and more boisterous, the better. He had a special pocket in his vest in which he kept candy or sugar cubes just for his young friends. Grandpa and Elaine would work together in the garden or, if it was hot, sit in the porch swing and talk. He would tell tales of his childhood in California's gold rush counties. He recounted stories he had heard from the old men when he was a boy. He talked about the Chinese, both those in California during the gold rush, and those who came later to work on the railroad. The Chinese he described seemed so different from the ones Elaine knew at school. She loved to hear him speak the Chinese phrases he had learned as a boy. She especially liked the stories he told of his father, her great-grandfather, a miner who wore a gun on each hip and played the violin. Grandpa told of the summer he had gone with his father to round up unbranded cattle left over from when California belonged to Spain and then Mexico. He told of chasing the cattle all over the San Joaquin Valley before rounding up enough to drive to the railhead in Fresno to sell. It was just like the western movies she sometimes saw at the Tower Theater on Saturdays.

Grandpa was a section foreman for the Southern Pacific Railroad. He was in charge of several miles of track. It was his responsibility to ensure that this section of track and the roadbed that supported it was always in good repair. He led a crew of men called "Braceros", which was a name for Mexicans who had come to the United States to work. The U.S. government had given them permission to be in the country just to work on the railroad. Grandpa took good care of his men. He had learned Spanish so that he could talk with them. From time to time, Elaine would hear him telling her father about his men. He always called them "his men", like he was the general of an army or something. He told about how he helped his men with the problems that they had. These men were in a strange country, after all, and most of them didn't speak English.

When the family visited Elaine's grandparents, they often also visited the railroad yards. The kids loved to go to "the yards" to watch the little steam switch engines hurry back and forth, busily sorting the loaded boxcars, flat cars, hoppers, and tankers into complete trains. Everyone knew the train was finished when the switch engine added the caboose to the end. The caboose was a little red car with a windowed cupola on top. It had an important function. In the cupola sat two brakemen, each watching a different side of the train, particularly the wheels and axles, as the train went around curves. They were looking for "hot boxes", which is what they called overheated axles, or anything else that might derail the train. If there was a problem with the train, they would use flags to signal the engineer to stop the engine. The caboose was also an office, lunchroom, and bathroom for the train crew. It had its own smokestack to carry away the smoke from the small coal-burning stove that was used for cooking, and to keep the car comfortable for the men inside.

Grandpa seemed to know everyone at "the yards." Sometimes, as a favor for Grandpa, an engineer would let the kids into the locomotive, or a brakeman would let them into a caboose.

It was important that the track be kept smooth by good maintenance of the roadbed, so that the fruit would not be bounced around and get bruised. Grandpa was very proud of the prizes he had won for having the smoothest track on the Southern Pacific Rail Line. He had the framed certificates of excellence hanging on the wall of the bedroom he shared with his wife.

Grandpa disliked driving and preferred to walk to work. On his way to and from "the yards" he would chat with his neighbors, all of whom were truck farmers. Many of his neighbors were immigrants who'd been drawn to Fresno by a soil and climate similar to their homelands. Sometimes, in the evenings or on Sundays, neighbors would stop by and talk, or Grandpa and Elaine would walk together through the local neighborhood—a mix of small vegetable farms, orchards, and berry patches. Grandpa West would greet each neighbor in the neighbor's own language: Italian, Greek, Armenian, or Japanese. Then they would chat, in English, about the weather, the crops, their families, and local and world affairs. Grandpa valued their opinions and knowledge. From them he learned new secrets of gardening, and different ways of curing olives, pickling vegetables, and drying fruit. He would share his knowledge of things political and economic. The neighbors frequently shared their produce as well as their knowledge. The Wests were never short of fresh fruits and vegetables. Everyone loved Grandpa, and just walking with him made Elaine feel special.

One Saturday, Billy, Sara, and Elaine were left with Grandpa while their mother and grandmother went shopping. They were just getting ready to help Grandpa gather the eggs from the chicken coop when the doorbell rang. It was Mr. Tagawa, one of Grandpa's neighbors.

Elaine recognized him immediately. She had met Mr. Tagawa on one of their neighborhood walks. Mr. Tagawa was from Japan. He had lots of children. They flocked to the fence when Grandpa came by, hoping for the candy they knew he carried. One of the children was a girl, Miko, who was about Elaine's age. While the men talked and laughed over the fence,

Miko and Elaine talked and laughed through the fence. They talked about school, mostly. Both girls loved school. Both were in second grade. But in addition to regular elementary school, Miko went to a Japanese school on Saturdays. There, she spent the whole day learning to read and write Japanese. Elaine was impressed. Elaine's Sunday school was only an hour. Elaine had often wished that she and Miko could play without a fence between them, but she had never been invited into Miko's yard. She had invited Miko over to play with her at her grandfather's house many times, but Mr. Tagawa had always said "Not today."

Mr. Tagawa bowed to Grandfather from the doorway.

"Konnichiwa, my friend. Come in," said Grandpa as he bowed back.

Mr. Tagawa removed his shoes and stepped into the room. He had been cheerful the other times Elaine had seen him, but today he looked very upset.

"Sit down." Grandpa motioned to a chair. "Can I make you some tea or get you some water?"

"Thank you, no." answered Mr. Tagawa. "I have trouble, my friend, big trouble!"

Even through the heavily accented English, Elaine heard the pain and worry in his voice.

Grandpa motioned to the children. "Kids, go and play. We'll gather the eggs later."

Sara took Billy went outside. Elaine went into the bedroom. She shook out her jacks and started to play, but she could hear the men talking and she listened.

"What's the problem, my friend?" asked Grandpa.

"The government want lock us up. Send to Japan at end of war. They say we enemy. We not enemy. I come here young man. Work hard. Obey laws. Save money. Send for wife. We have five children here. Children not know Japan, never see Japan. We love America. My English bad. They English good but Japanese no good. They love school. Today they cry long time. They call name at school. My wife and I love America. We not know how new Japan make war."

There was silence. Finally Grandpa spoke, "I understand, my friend. Let me see what I can do. Let me call a lawyer friend. He may be able to help you. Wait here. The phone is in the kitchen."

Elaine could not hear her grandfather on the phone. As she resumed her jacks game, she thought about what she had heard. She knew the names they were calling Miko, the same names the third graders had called Jimmy. Were they beating her up as well?

After a while Grandpa came back to the living room and asked, "What documents do you have?" There was a long silence. "Birth certificates?" There was more silence. Mr. Tagawa didn't seem to understand. "You know...err... papers?"

"Ah, papers. Yes, I have papers when I come America," said Mr. Tagawa.

"Do you have papers for the children?"

"Children?" He paused. "No, no papers for children."

"Were they born in a hospital?" asked Grandpa.

"No. Born at home. Japanese way. No papers. Papers important?" asked Mr. Tagawa.

"You may not be a citizen, my friend," Grandpa said, "but your children are! They were born here and that automatically makes them citizens. They cannot be sent back to Japan. And since they are so young, you and your wife will be allowed to stay and take care of them. But we must get proof that they were born in the United States. I'll make another phone call."

Grandpa went back into the kitchen, and Elaine went back to her jacks game. She felt proud of her Grandpa. He always helped people, always made things better.

When Grandpa returned, he told Mr. Tagawa of the arrangements he had made to swear out birth certificates for the Tagawa children.

Once Mr. Tagawa was gone, Grandpa called all of us into the living room. "Sit down, children!" he said. He looked at each child in turn. He wanted them to know that what he had to say was very important. "I want you to listen very carefully. This war is not the fault of the Tagawas. This war is the fault of the Japs, the Nazis, and the Fascists. The Tagawas are not Japs any more than my neighbor Mr. Rossi is a Fascist or your neighbor Mr. Schultz is a Nazi. Being Japanese does not make you a Jap, being Italian doesn't not make you a Fascist, and being German does not make you a Nazi! People should answer for their own deeds and not those of their county, especially if they no longer live there. Never forget that!"

"Will Mr. Tagawa and Miko be alright?" Elaine asked.

"I hope so!" said Grandpa, "But there is a lot of unthinking hatred during wartime. Innocent people suffer."

He paused. When he spoke again his tone had changed. "Now, let's go gather those eggs." He took Billy's hand and strode off.

Sara, who had not overheard anything, whispered to Elaine, "What was that all about?"

"The Tagawas are in deep trouble over the war." Elaine answered, and whispered the details to her on the way to the chicken coop. Elaine was delighted that for once she knew more than Sara did.

In the car on the way home Elaine was thinking about what Grandpa had said about the Fascists, the Nazis, and the Japs. They were the enemy. "Mother, are the Schultzes Germans?"

"I suppose so. They were born in Germany, but they've lived here a long time. And their son, Frank, was born here."

Elaine had always liked the Schultzes, Frank especially. Even though he was a teacher at the high school, he always talked to her like she was a grownup and not just a silly child.

"I just thought that they were Americans who talked funny," said Elaine. So many people had come to California from so many different places—Oklahoma, New Jersey, Italy, and Greece. Elaine was used to people who talked funny.

"Well they've sort of adopted America as their country. They never had plans to go back to Germany."

Elaine would have liked to ask more questions, but Mother and Father were talking to each other now, and Elaine knew better than to interrupt.

CHAPTER 7

March, 1942

Winter was turning into spring. The War was going badly for the Allies. The United States, Britain, China, Australia and others were losing men, ships, and supplies in their battles with the Axis Powers of Germany, Italy, and Japan. But the action was far away—the Japanese had not yet bombed California. And so, while people didn't feel safe, exactly, they at least felt prepared. People in Fresno were still alert, but no longer in a panic.

It was Saturday and the neighborhood children were playing at the Wests' house as usual. The drone of an engine rolled in from the sky, growing louder with each passing second. The kids paused in their play. All eyes turned skyward.

"It sounds like a B24," yelled Tommy. The others scanned the sky quickly locating the plane easily by the burr of its engines.

"No, it's a C47," countered Rae Dean, as the plane grew closer.

"It's a B24!" insisted Tommy.

"No, a C47!"

"A C47 only has two engines," said Tommy. "This one has four. It has to be a B24."

"You're both wrong," said Sara, amused at their lack of skill in airplane identification. "It's a B17!" She was the oldest, so that settled the matter.

It was an unusually warm spring day. The kids were in the back yard, playing war as they often did. Tommy was flying a P36. Elaine was getting ready for take off in a P40 fighter. Billy and Rae Dean were behind different bushes, manning their broomstick anti-aircraft guns. Sara was in the control tower located in the fig tree. The planes were swings that Father had built in the backyard. They were wonderfully tall, taller than the swings in the schoolyard, taller even than the swings in the park. They had flat wooden seats supported by soft ropes. They were the envy of the neighborhood.

"This is Blue Fox requesting clearance for takeoff, over," Elaine called in her best radio voice.

"All clear, Blue Fox. Over and out." Sara replied in her capacity as air traffic controller.

"Roger and Out. Ehnerrrrrr!" Elaine revved up her engines for takeoff.

The kids all knew the sounds of aerial warfare. Every afternoon at 4:30 the West children, like most children, huddled around the radio in the living room to listen to *Captain Midnight* and then *Sky King*. Father didn't like it when they listened to these "blood and thunder" shows, but they always did anyway. From the radio they could here the roar of engines and propellers, the terrible "ack-ack-ack-ack" of machine gun fire, and the shouted reports and commands of the men in the cockpits. The sights of aerial warfare, on the other hand, had to be imagined. Mother wouldn't let them watch war movies because she thought those movies were too violent. Movie newsreels didn't show real combat footage. Government censors, who decided what could and could not be shown, were afraid real combat footage might give information to enemy spies.

As Army Air Corps pilot Blue Fox, Elaine piloted her swing. She pumped hard with her legs to gain altitude as her favorite fighting song played in her head like a phonograph record…

> *"Off we go into the wild blue yonder*
> *Climbing high into the sun.*
> *Down we dive firing our guns like thunder*
> *At 'em boys! Give 'em the gun!*
> *We will live in fame*
> *Or go down in flame.*
> *Nothing can stop the Army Air Corps."*

Elaine went higher and higher, climbing and swooping as her airplane swing flew into the air.

"Zero at 9:00 o'clock," Tommy radioed Elaine from the neighboring swing. It was a Jap fighter, closing in from her left side.

"I see him. Let's get him!"

"Another's on your tail!"

"I've been hit!" Elaine wailed. "I'm going into a spin!" She jerked the swing rope hard to the right and threw her body and legs into a turn.

Slowly the swing ropes twisted. "I can't straighten it out! I'm out of control! I'd better hit the silk."

"Elaine, we're not supposed to jump out of the swings!" Sara scolded.

Elaine was jolted out of her fantasy, if only for the moment. 'Why does she always have to be like that?' she thought. But Sara was too late anyways. Elaine was already out of the swing and heading for the ground.

"Ack! Ack! Ack! I got him for you 'Laine!" yelled Billy proudly. "Scratch one Zero."

Almost instantly, Elaine was readying for another take off.

"Hey! I see a convoy coming!" yelled Sara from her perch in the fig tree. Elaine pushed forward on the swing ropes. "Where is it, Control? I'll strafe it."

"No, I mean a *real* convoy. It's coming down our street."

This time Sara didn't notice when Elaine bailed out of the swing and rushed to the sidewalk with the other kids to watch the convoy go by. First came the jeeps.

"One, two, three, four, five, six, seven, eight," Billy counted as the jeeps went by in single file, one after another. Each jeep's bumper was only a couple of feet from the rear bumper of the jeep in front of it.

"It's going to be a long one!" Tommy's voice rang out.

"Did you see that fellow in the second jeep, the one who smiled and waved?" asked Rae Dean.

"Most of them smile and wave," said Sara.

"But this one looked like my uncle George. Do you think it could be him?" Rae Dean was not sure.

"Where is your uncle George?" Elaine asked.

"I don' know. Somebody—mom calls him the censor—goes through his mail so we can't see all the words. Every time he writes a place the censor covers it with thick black ink."

"That means he's overseas somewhere," said Sara.

"How do you know?"

"'Cause they only censor the overseas mail, or the mail that talks about going overseas. That way the enemy can't find out where our troops are. So you see, that couldn't have been him. He's out of the country."

"Well maybe he's just goin' overseas. Maybe this whole convoy is full o' men going overseas." Elaine had learned not to start arguments with Sara, but Rae Dean hadn't and Rae Dean could be very stubborn.

"It wasn't your uncle. I'd bet you a quarter!" Sara responded.

"Look! Here come the trucks." Billy was jumping up and down with excitement. Huge khaki covered army trucks began to roll slowly by, one after another, with only inches between them. "I wonder what's inside of 'em. Guns?"

"I'll bet it's men," Rae Dean insisted.

"It's probably just food." Sara was ever practical.

"Let's count the trucks," suggested Tommy.

"No, it's too late. We've already missed ten or fifteen of them," It was Sara again, pointing out realities. "Besides, last time we tried to count them you all got bored and left before we even got to a hundred."

"Look!" Billy cried. "That one's open. It's got soldiers in it! They're waving!"

"See?" Rae Dean said pointedly, "I told you it was men."

Truck after truck rolled slowly by. Many had the canvas sides pulled up like flaps on a tent. All the open trucks had soldiers in them. Lots of the men waved.

"There are six soldiers in a truck," said Billy. "I counted 'em!"
Billy was very proud of his counting ability.

"Actually, there are twelve. There are six more men on the other side of the truck, but you can't see them." Sara spoke with certainty.

"If the trucks weren't so close together we could cross the street and see if she's right." proposed Rae Dean.

"She's probably right. It makes sense that if there are men on this side, there are men on the other side too." Elaine knew that Sara usually had her facts straight.

"I know I'm right," Sara said. "Ask anybody."

Truck after truck rolled by.

"You know, some of the kids in my Sunday school class have never seen a convoy." Elaine said. Nobody was listening, but she didn't let that stop her. She often had whole conversations with no one in particular. "I had to explain that a convoy is just one army truck or jeep after another going down the road. They didn't believe me when I told them that they don't stop for anything. Not even stop signs or red lights."

"Yeah, we're real lucky that when convoys go through town they go down the street by our house," said Sara.

"Why?" asked Billy.

"Because the highway goes through the center of town. Convoys would really tie up the traffic if they went that way." explained Sara.

"But why our street?" he insisted.

"Oh, you wouldn't understand."

Sara said that a lot to Billy and Elaine. Elaine thought it was Sara's way of saying that she didn't know. Still, Elaine knew better than to call her on it.

"I wonder where they come from?" asked Tommy.

"From the highway, silly!" put in Rae Dean.

"No, I mean before the highway?"

Sara sighed. "You just wouldn't understand." Now, Elaine was *sure* it was Sara's way of saying she didn't know.

"I don't know where they came from, but I know where they're going," Elaine was always pleased to show off her knowledge. "To the docks, leastwise that's what Mother says. She says most of what is needed to fight the Japanese—that doesn't get carried by the railroads—goes on trucks, right by our house and down the highway to the docks."

"And from there it's loaded onto Navy ships," Sara added, "and carried across San Francisco Bay and out through the Golden Gate to the War in the Pacific." Sara, too, had heard the explanation.

"No wonder there are so many trucks!" sighed Tommy.

"I've seen enough of 'em," said Billy. "Let's go play war. This time, I want to be a pilot!" Billy ran and jumped into a swing. "Somebody push me!"

The diversion over, the kids were back to playing war.

"Sara, Elaine, Billy!" Mother called from the doorway. "Your Grandpa's here."

The West kids abandoned their playmates and the game and hurried into the house. Grandpa was indeed there in the kitchen.

"Where's Grandma?" asked Sara.

"She'll be back soon, explained Grandpa. "She just dropped me off here with these while she did some shopping." His hand indicated the large wooden strawberry box sitting on the kitchen table. "Alice," he continued, "would you like these?"

Mother began to remove the contents of the box and set them on the table. Elaine caught her breath. The box contained dishes but they were unlike any dishes she had ever seen before. These dishes were not white or painted in soft pinks, blues, and greens. These were brown and cream, and painted in vivid shades of orange, black, purple, red and dark forest green. They were trimmed with what looked like real gold. Elaine recognized some of the scenes from the pictures in *Little Stories and Pictures of Japan*, a book Mother had sometimes read to them. The small plates and cups were decorated with pictures of Japanese Samurai, mounted on fiery stallions. The teapot was fantastic. It was a fat dragon with a tail of raised gilded scales for a handle. On the other side, a dragon neck made a spout, and Elaine could imagine steaming hot tea spilling out from the dragon's mouth. The sugar bowl and cream pitcher were painted with beautiful kimono-clad women smiling under brightly colored parasols. Elaine looked closer and saw how even the tiny fans in the women's hands were and painted with exquisite detail. The whole set was breathtaking!

"Don't you want these?" Mother asked with bewilderment. Elaine could tell that Mother, too, thought the dishes were beautiful.

"I do!" said grandpa sadly, "But Sadie doesn't." Sarah was Grandmother's given name, but most people called her Sadie. "She says they're ugly heathen things and she doesn't want them in the house. Make some tea, please, and I'll enjoy them here."

"However did you come by them?" asked Mother

"They were on my porch this morning," replied Grandpa. "There was no note with them, but I have a pretty good idea of where they came from. You know my Japanese neighbors? About two weeks back, Mr. Tagawa—

that's the family name, Tagawa—was in trouble with the government. To help him, Mr. Napolitano—you know, my neighbor who grows those large peaches—well, Mr. Napolitano and I went down to the courthouse and swore out birth certificates for Mr. Tagawa's children. We didn't witness the births of course, but we could swear that the Togawas were here when they happened. We figured that once the children were recognized as U.S. citizens, the government would have to leave him alone. So when I found the dishes on the porch this morning, I hurried off to thank the Tagawas, but they were gone! None of the neighbors saw them leave, some didn't even know they were gone, but one said he'd seen an Army truck when he got up at dawn to do some milking." Grandpa paused, and then said quietly, "I think the government's taken them away. I think they were interned."

'Interned'. It sounded so frightening. Elaine was alarmed yet puzzled. "Interned, what's that?"

"It's sort of like being put in prison, except the whole family can go and live there together," Mother explained. She said it like it was something sad and terrible.

Imprisoned, the whole family. Elaine couldn't understand it; she thought of Miko and her brothers and sisters, and it made her afraid. "But why...what happens to them now?"

"Elaine, we're at war now. And a lot goes on when there's a war that we are never told, and even when we are told we don't necessarily understand." Mother's voice was sad. She sighed. "You girls get these beautiful dishes washed while I boil some water and then we'll brew some tea."

Sara and Elaine proceeded into the kitchen, and Sara got out the dishpan. "These dishes look new, and the cups are large like our dishes, not small like cups in that Chinese restaurant we go to sometimes." Sara remarked.

"They must have been bought as a gift," said Mother.

By the time the water boiled, the dishes were ready to use. While the tea steeped in the dragon teapot, Mother set a plate of cookies on the table. When the tea was ready, she poured each person a cup. The steaming tea came out of the dragon's mouth as the dragon's beady gold eyes watched.

As Elaine sipped her tea and nibbled on a cookie, she noticed the strawberry box the dishes had come in. It reminded her of the strawberry fields they had passed the last time they had all driven out to visit her grandparents. She thought of Mr. Tagawa and the other Japanese farmers who had grown strawberries. She thought about how every year, in the early spring, Mr. Tagawa covered each small plant every evening with a small white paper cap to protect it from the cold night air. Each morning he removed the cap so the plant could warm itself in the sun. She had seen him removing the caps when they went early to visit her grandparents. Sometimes, his wife and older children were helping him. Elaine thought about Miko pulling the caps off the strawberry plants and stacking them neatly in her other hand. Elaine remembered how the not-yet-collected white caps had made a beautiful pattern against the brown soil, as did the dark green dots of the tiny young plants that had already been uncovered. What would become of the Tagawas' strawberries now? Of the Tagawas themselves? Of Miko?

CHAPTER 8

April, 1942

Weeks had passed, and there was still no word of the Tagawas. Soon after they disappeared, an Italian family moved into their house, plowed up the strawberries and planted tomatoes.

The radio news was always on in the kitchen when Elaine and Sara went in to help Mother with breakfast. Ever since Pearl Harbor, the radio had never been off during the day—not once—though often the volume was turned low. Mother and Father wanted to get the latest news of the War, hoping to hear that our forces had won a victory. But news of the War was never good. It was always about this place or that place surrendering to the Japanese. More and more the Pacific Ocean was becoming a Japanese lake. Many of the kids at Sara and Elaine's school had relatives in the National Guard, which had been called up and sent to defend the Philippines against the Japanese attack. These men had been trained to fight forest fires, find lost children, and keep the irrigation canals from flooding when there was a heavy rain or a sudden snowmelt in the mountains. Now, they found themselves fighting the Japanese Regular Army. It was a hard, bloody fight, against an enemy that had been hardened by years of war in China and Southeast Asia. Almost every week, one of Elaine's classmates was notified that a relative or family friend had been killed or badly injured in the Philippines.

One evening, Elaine was playing jacks in her favorite corner of the living room when Father suddenly turned up the volume on the radio. "Alice, you'll want to hear this!" he called.

As Mother walked in the newscaster repeated: "Allied forces in the Pacific suffered their largest defeat of the war to date, as the Army of Imperial Japan launched an assault on American forces stationed along the Bataan Peninsula in the Philippines. The U.S. Army estimates that over 20,000 Allied troops were either killed or captured in the attack."

"Fresno's National Guard is a part of that force!" Mother exclaimed. "All those men! What will happen to them?"

"I don't know." Father slowly shook his head. "By all accounts, the Japanese don't treat prisoners well."

Elaine wanted to ask questions, but it was clear now was not the time. And from the sound of their voices, neither Mother nor Father would be reassuring. Both just sat there for some time, staring into space. Elaine went to the globe that sat on the end table next to the sofa. She studied the globe. Japan was so tiny. Not even as big as Texas. How could it continue to beat Britain, China, the United States and all the other countries that together made up the Allies?

Maybe Sara was right. Maybe Elaine just didn't understand.

After school that day, Rae Dean came rushing over. She was breathless. She had obviously been running. "Guess what! We finally heard from my dad an' he's okay, not hurt or anything, an' he's joined the Navy so he could write to us 'cus there's no civilian mail, 'an now he's a Sea Bee, so he's still working construction." She finally stopped for air.

"What's a Sea Bee?' asked Elaine, trying to make sense of what Rae Dean had just said.

"It's part of the Navy. An' they build stuff. Their real name is Naval Construction Brigade, but everybody just calls 'em the Sea Bees 'cus their initials are C. B. 'an they're always buzzing around like busy bees."

"I'm so pleased to hear that he's all right," said Mother.

"Yeah, me too." echoed Sara.

"I may be a sea bee when I grow up." Billy was not yet old enough to go to school. He almost never talked, but he could already read and count. He was always around though. When he did speak it was clear that he knew what was going on.

"Since you're here, would you like to stay for supper, Rae Dean?" Mother asked. "We're having meat loaf, mashed potatoes, and green beans."

"You bet. Can I use the phone to call my mother an' ask?" Elaine noticed that Mother didn't insist she say "*may* I use the phone."

After dinner Rae Dean, Sara, and Elaine had finished the dishes and were getting ready to play rummy in the kitchen. They had the smaller radio on, and were listening to *Jack Benny* while they played.

But then the radio went dead. Sara was investigating why it would no longer play when Mother came in. "Put your game away," she said. "We're going to have an air-raid drill."

As soon as she said it, the siren on the telephone pole outside began to howl. "How did you know?" Rae Dean turned to Mother.

"The radio went off the air. It always does during an air-raid drill, because air planes can navigate using radio signals coming from the ground."

A silent radio was the first hint of an air raid or drill. Neither Elaine nor anybody else ever knew if it was a drill or the real thing until it was over. That winter and spring, the people of Fresno practiced hiding in the dark on a fairly regular basis, especially when the weather was good for flying, and the moon was full or nearly full.

"Girls, quickly, find Billy, get out the books you want me to read to you, and then go into the living room."

"I'd better go home," said Rae Dean.

"No, you'll have to stay. No one is allowed outside during a drill unless they have a special job to do, like policemen and firemen."

"Then I'd better phone." Rae Dean did not want her mother to worry.

"No, child. We are not supposed to use the phone except for emergencies. Your mother knows where you are. When it's over, Mr. West will walk you home."

Mother folded lengths of heavy black muslin over the curtain rods, which had been extended beyond the windows for that purpose. Only the living and dining room windows had these curtains—"blackout curtains", Mother called them—and so, whenever there was a drill, these were the only rooms that were used. "Use the bathroom now. You won't be able to use it with the light on again until the drill is over," Mother directed. "Sara, go through the rest of the house and make sure all the lights are off. Even if this is a real raid, there should be time. If an enemy plane were spotted on the seacoast, it would take at least half an hour before it could get to Fresno. Still, we should hurry just in case the plane was spotted late."

Once the house was ready, everyone gathered on the living room sofa, or on the floor in front of it. There, Mother prepared to read to them by the light of a single lamp.

Father put on a white hard hat marked with a red "CD" in a blue triangle and put on a matching armband. The "CD" stood for civil defense.

He took a specially dimmed flashlight, a shovel, and a bucket of sand and went out into the night.

"Where's he going?" asked Rae Dean. "I thought no one was allowed out on the streets."

"He has a job. He's the block warden. He has to check for anything out of the ordinary, and he has to make sure no light is showing," said Elaine. "He even checks the Creamery."

"Is it dark in the Creamery?" asked Billy. Billy loved the Creamery down the street. It was the source of ice cream.

"No. They have blackout shades just like we do. Any public building open after dark has blackout shades," explained Mother. "The customers just can't open the door and leave until the all clear."

"How awful to be stuck in the Creamery!" Sara giggled at her own joke.

"Yeah, just think of all the ice cream you'd have to eat." laughed Elaine.

"Why did he take the bucket of sand an' the shovel?" Rae Dean asked.

"So he can put out any fire started by a bomb," Elaine answered.

"An' the flashlight? I thought no light was allowed in a blackout."

"It's a special "CD" flashlight. It has a blue lens on it because blue light is hard to see from the air." Mother explained.

Her questions answered, Rae Dean settled down to listen to Mother read. After the first story, Billy had to use the bathroom, in spite of Mother's telling him to use it earlier. Sara went with him because the bathroom was in the dark part of the house. Rae Dean thought that would be fun so when Billy came back she asked to go. Elaine was only too happy to take her into the dark part of the house to use the bathroom too. When everyone settled down, Mother started another story. She was on her third story and Billy was asleep in her lap when the all clear sounded. The radio came back on and announced that it had only been a drill, and that it was over. Soon Father came home. He took off his helmet and armband, and then walked Rae Dean to her house.

Elaine loved air raid drills because there was a longer story time and they got to stay up late. She also thought they were scary, in a Halloween sort of way that is—exciting, and even fun!

Father left for work the next Monday and was home again before the children had left for school. "Now that the snow in the mountains has started to melt, the Army is sending me to a place in the northeast corner of California, a place called Tule Lake. I just came home to pack a bag and to leave the car."

"How long will you be gone?" asked Mother.

"They didn't say, but I don't have much time to pack. They're sending a jeep after me."

"What if we have an air raid drill while you're gone?"

"I told the officer I was a block warden. I was hoping he'd decide to send someone else. But no such luck. He said they'd take care of that detail. The Army needed me in Tule Lake."

"For what?"

"To survey some land. He didn't say what for."

Sara and Elaine said goodbye to Father and headed to school, not knowing when they would see him again.

CHAPTER 9

May, 1942

Three weeks later, early on a Saturday morning, Billy rushed into the girls' bedroom yelling, "Daddy's home! Daddy's home! I saw his stuff."

Mother rushed in. "Shh! Shh!' she hissed, finger to her lip. "Don't wake him up. He's sick."

"What's he got?" There was worry in Sara's voice.

"Just a bad cold, I think. He's been working from sun up to sun down, sleeping in a tent, and eating Army food. He's too old for that."

"But he's home now. He'll be able to rest up," said Sara.

"Only until Monday. A jeep will pick him up at 4:00 A.M."

"But if he's sick?"

"The Army doesn't care. There is a war on."

"But what's he doing?" asked Elaine.

"You children know you're not to talk about it if I tell you?" said Mother.

"Is it a secret?" asked Billy

"No. If it were a secret I wouldn't know it, but it's best just not to talk about whatever the Army does."

"We know," said Elaine. "Our teachers are always telling us that. And then there's that poster that says "Loose Lips Sink Ships!" So what is it he's doing?"

"He is surveying for an enemy alien internment camp the Army is building," Mother explained. "It'll be a place to put the Japanese people who the government thinks might help Japan."

"You mean spies?" Elaine asked.

"Well, they might be spies, they might just be Japanese who send money to relatives in Japan, or send their children to Japanese school, or do any one of another things that makes the Army suspicious."

51

"Like the Tagawas? Miko went to Japanese school." Elaine had not thought about Miko for a long while. "What's the camp like?"

"Your father says it will have little shacks for houses and a barbed wire fence with guard towers."

"Sounds like a prison. Is that what happened to the Tagawas?"

"We don't know that the Tagawas were interned," said Mother. "They may have just moved." Elaine knew from Mother's voice that she didn't think that was what had really happened. "Come on, let's eat breakfast."

Elaine knew that was all Mother was going to say on the subject.

Monday morning Father, still suffering from his cold, left at dawn to return to Tule Lake. After all, there was a war on.

With every American defeat in the Pacific, and every rumor of mistreatment of American prisoners and civilians by the Japanese Army, hatred of all things Japanese grew. People came to believe that the Japanese were less than human. Acts of vandalism and even violence against the Japanese people living on the West Coast increased. Although there was no proof that the Japanese were not loyal Americans, the government chose to bow to public opinion. People in the government decided that all people of Japanese ancestry, even American citizens, were to be relocated away from the Pacific Ocean. *Relocated*, such a gentle word for what happened. Whole families were forced to leave their homes, farms, and businesses. They were given very little time to prepare to leave. There was not enough time to sell what they owned for a fair price, and each person was allowed to take only one small suitcase. Everything else—cars, furniture, livestock, and even pets—they were forced to give away, leave behind, or put in government storage. Those Japanese living around Fresno were told to go to the Fresno County Fair Grounds and wait there for further orders.

Father's cold didn't get better. In fact, it just kept getting worse. Finally, it got so bad that the Army sent him back to Fresno. They couldn't really afford to lose such a talented engineer, but if he stayed in the mountains and developed pneumonia, there would be nobody to treat him, as all the doctors were treating servicemen overseas.

And so, Father continued his work on the camp by mail. Every day, he would assemble the survey notes that had been sent to him from the site, and mail the plans back to Tule Lake. He still worked long days, but now he came home each night, which was a welcome change for the family. One evening, after Elaine had gone to bed, she overheard him talking to Mother.

"Alice, they've started herding Japanese families into the fairgrounds. They've filled the exhibition halls, and were filling up the livestock barns by the time I left."

"Who's in charge of this relocation?" asked Mother.

"Seems to be the Army. At least, there were lots of Army guards there so the Japanese wouldn't run away. Although, I don't know where the Army thinks they'd go. There are hundreds of them: men, women, old people, children, even babies. As I was leaving it started to rain. Everyone looked so miserable."

"It sounds terrible. How long are the Japanese going to be there?"

"No one seems to know."

"It all seems terribly unfair," said Mother. "I sometimes wonder if this whole relocation business isn't the result of a plot by the California Fruit Growers' Association to get rid of competition. They've resented the Japanese farmers for years because they grow better fruit."

Elaine, who had gone to the fair the fall, tried to remember what the buildings at the fair grounds were like. What she remembered best was standing in a long line to use the bathroom. There was no hot water. How could people bathe? She pictured the animal barns in her mind. They had tall tin roofs, but the outside walls weren't solid and the windows had no glass in them. It was nice that way in the heat of September, because it let the breezes in and the smells out. But in May? It was still cold at night. She hoped they had lots of blankets. She hoped they had beds for that matter. At the fair the floors had been covered with straw. Was there dirt or concrete under the straw? Elaine couldn't remember. She tried to imagine people living at the fairgrounds. It just didn't seem like the sort of place she would ever want to live.

Elaine lay awake for a long time that night, wondering about the Tagawas. She wondered if the Tagawas were at the fairgrounds, or maybe in a relocation camp already. Or maybe they were somewhere else, waiting to be sent to Tule Lake? If they were waiting, she hoped it wasn't in an animal barn. From what her father said, Tule Lake sounded like it would be a terrible place, just groups of tiny thin-walled houses sitting in the dirt.

When the buildings were finished, the whole camp was to be surrounded by a barbed wire fence with guard towers, like a prison. It would be better than animal barns, but not by much.

Eventually, Elaine drifted off to sleep.

CHAPTER 10

June, 1942

Summer was coming on, and still the Allies were losing. In Europe, German planes began targeting cities in the British countryside, terrifying civilians and destroying centuries-old cathedrals. In the Pacific, island after island fell under Japanese control, and the rumors leaking out from the front told stories of mass murder, torture, and starvation. Supply lines were cut, and mail rarely got through.

At home, too, it was becoming hard to find some food items—such as sugar, chocolate, coffee, tea, and even meat—in the stores. To force people to share foods that were in short supply, the government issued ration books. Everybody got a ration book, even tiny children. Each book had the name of the owner, already typed on the cover. Ration books were small, not much bigger than a few playing cards. Most of the pages were full of red or blue stamps, about half the size of the smallest postage stamp. There was a number on each stamp to tell how many "points" it was worth. When a person bought rationed items, such as meat, butter, coffee, canned and dried foods, and sugar, he or she had to pay for each item with ration points as well as money. A customer even had to use ration stamps to get some foods in a restaurant.

Shoes were rationed too. Soldiers wore shoes out rapidly, and the shoe factories were making shoes not only for American soldiers, but also for British, Chinese, Russian, and other allied soldiers. Gasoline was rationed as well. In fact, that ration was so small that everybody walked or took the bus whenever they could. The Wests' semiweekly drive to the branch library eight blocks away became a semiweekly walk. They almost never went downtown. When they did, they took the bus. Stores and businesses were closing, as there was little to sell, and the people who used to work in the stores had either joined the military or were needed for war work.

Automobiles, furniture, stoves, refrigerators, and even toys were no longer being made. The factories had all re-tooled to make weapons. There were plenty of jobs and not enough workers. This seemed strange to Elaine, because for as long as she could remember, she had heard stories of the Great Depression, when there were lots of workers, like Father, who couldn't find jobs. Posters went up all over town, asking women to go to work in the factories making war goods. Everyone had money, but there was little to buy. It was almost impossible to get anything fixed. Repair shops closed as the repairmen went off to war. People were expected to make do with what they had. Wearing last year's clothes became patriotic. Grandmother made the children's clothes out of whatever cloth she could find in the stores, or cut from used adult clothing. Hemlines rose to above the knees and men's pants no longer had cuffs as everyone tried to save cloth.

May came and went. From his office at the fairgrounds, Father finally completed his work on the camp at Tule Lake. The Japanese were still at the fairgrounds, but it was expected that they would be leaving soon. Father bought a used bicycle to ride to work. Nobody ever rode it for fun. Father was very careful with the bicycle tires, because rubber was impossible to come by. He even hung the bike up when he was not riding it so there was no weight on the tires. He was saving the family's gasoline ration, and the tires on the 1941 Chevrolet, so the family could use the car to go on vacation. They were fortunate to have a new car, as cars were no longer being made, and older cars, if they broke down, were almost impossible to get fixed.

Many kids, like Rae Dean, never saw their fathers anymore. Sara and Elaine knew they were lucky to see theirs every evening. With Father home regularly now, the Wests resumed having servicemen as guests for Sunday dinner. Mother would get a chicken or two from Grandpa and use some of the family's precious ration stamps to give the airmen the best home cooked meal she could. Elaine really enjoyed these Sundays. But she came to understand that these airmen were only temporary friends. Each man came only once, twice, maybe three times at most. Then he shipped out to the War in the Pacific. No longer were these young men in a hurry to go off to war and "teach the Japs a lesson." Now they knew that the war would be long and hard. The motto was "Golden Gate by '48" meaning that they hoped that the war would be won by 1948 so they could sail home through San Francisco's Golden Gate, under its famous bridge.

No one ever even considered the possibility that America might lose.

I was the first Saturday in June when Elaine woke up to the sound of the radio, and heard Mother and Father excitedly chattering in the kitchen. She hurried in to see what they were so excited about. On the kitchen table lay that morning's newspaper. The headline took up the whole front page. **"VICTORY at MIDWAY! 4 JAP CARRIERS SUNK!"**

"Where's Midway?" asked Elaine.

"In the Pacific. Our Navy has just sunk the carriers that attacked Pearl Harbor." Mother answered.

"Does this mean we're winning the War?" asked Elaine.

"At the very least we've crippled the Japanese Navy!" Father was more excited than Elaine could ever remember his being.

Fourth of July that year, 1942, was the happiest Elaine could remember. The Wests' church had a huge Sunday school picnic in Roeding Park. There were relays, sack races, three legged races, and wheelbarrow races for the kids. The women lined up for an egg toss and the men had a tug of war. There were many men in uniform at the picnic who joined in the games. Some of the airmen paired off with the older girls, those out of high school, and wandered around the park. They particularly seemed to enjoy strolling two by two through the twisting, winding tunnel of the nearby grape arbor. When the airmen weren't chasing the girls, all they could talk about was the victory at Midway. The war might not last as long as they had thought. Instead of "Golden Gate by '48," their hope now was "Home Alive in '45."

Everyone had brought food to share. People with large gardens had brought watermelons and laid them on the grass in the deepest shade they could find. They covered them with wet gunnysacks. The men periodically drenched them with water from a bucket to keep them wet. The water on the sacks evaporated in the dry heat and cooled the melons. By suppertime the melons were cold. For dessert there was ice cream that came packed in dry ice to keep it from melting. The younger children were amazed by the way the dry ice seemed to burn their fingers and steamed and fizzled when it got wet. The older children knew what to expect. Each of the kids picked up a chip and quickly dropped it into an empty ice cream cup, then added water. The dry ice crackled, popped, fizzed and smoked. Elaine like playing with the dry ice better than eating the ice cream.

After dinner, the kids organized a huge game of "Kick the Can." Their game became ever more fun as the shadows deepened and darkness approached. The older kids and young adults spent more and more time in the grape arbor as the light dimmed. The kids all wondered what they were doing in there, but the adults made them stay away. When the light was gone, the picnic ended. The electric lights in the park stayed off. It was a reminder that, despite Midway, the war was still on.

CHAPTER 11

July, 1942

Summer was always hot in Fresno. By mid-July it was so hot during the day that by mid-afternoon the asphalt on the street in front of the Wests' house was soft to the touch. The temperature had risen above one hundred degrees every day for over a week. Elaine could hardly wait until the next Saturday, when the family would go on vacation. The Army had given Father a whole week off.

The family needed a vacation. So much had changed since Pearl Harbor. Even after Midway the War made everyone extra tense, on edge. Father, particularly, was under a lot of strain. He was home so seldom that Mother did her best to keep the children from annoying him. This was especially hard with Elaine, who seemed to annoy Father with everything she did and especially what she said. The whole family needed a rest from the strain and the heat. They also needed a rest from the War.

Mother and Father had decided to spend the week at Grandmother and Grandpa's cabin near Santa Cruz. Santa Cruz was a fun place. It was the favorite vacation place for Northern California. People went there to fish and swim in the Pacific Ocean, play, or just lounge about on the beautiful beach, or enjoy the never-ending carnival on the boardwalk next to the beach.

The cabin was near Felton, a tiny town in the nearby hills. It sat deep in the thick damp shade of a redwood forest. It was always cool there, cool enough to need a fire in summertime. Grandmother had driven over there weeks ago. She always spent the whole summer there. Grandpa had managed to get vacation from the railroad for the same week as Father's vacation. He would drive over with the family.

Mother and Father were talking about the trip one evening at the dinner table. The children were there too, but they had grown up with the knowledge that they were not part of the conversation. Father had always said, "When adults talk to each other, children are to be seen and not heard."

"Alice, I'm afraid we'll have to make the trip at night."

"But, John, it will be dark by the time we get over the mountains." There was worry in Mother's voice. "On the coast there is always a blackout."

Elaine wondered how many of the rooms had blackout curtains in the cabin. Would she be allowed a nightlight? What about a light in the bathroom? It was hard enough not doing anything to upset Grandma, but to do it in the dark! She looked across the table at Father.

"I know. We'll have to drive with dimmed lights," he said. "But I'm afraid the tires won't stand up to the heat of the day. At night the blacktop will be cool."

"But the dimmers only let a tiny bit of blue light show." Mother was still worried.

"There'll be very little traffic and the moon will be nearly full. It should be safe enough. I know the road so well."

A night trip sounded great to Elaine. The car would be crowded with Grandpa, the parents, and three children. It would be much more comfortable at night, when it was cooler. They made this trip every year and she remembered it as long and boring. After dark, she could sleep in the backseat while Father drove.

The following Friday evening, they ate a quick supper immediately after Father got home from work on his bicycle. The car was already packed and waiting in the driveway. It was stuffed. The excess baggage was tied on the outside and on the top. Father was happier than Elaine had seen him in a long time.

Five o'clock is the hottest time of the day in Fresno, but after that, the temperature drops quickly. It was a little after six o'clock by the time the Wests got to the highway. Elaine checked the temperature just before they left. It had already fallen to eighty-five degrees. As they drove, oleander bushes and strong smelling eucalyptus trees shaded the two-lane highway. With the car windows down, it was warm but not too unpleasant in the crowded back seat, even in the middle where Elaine was sitting.

Elaine always had to sit in the middle, especially on long trips, because Sara and Billy would quarrel otherwise. This whole arrangement seemed very unfair to her, as she felt like she was being punished because Sara and Billy couldn't behave. But Mother insisted, so Elaine had gotten used to it.

The kids were free to do pretty much as they pleased in the back seat as long as they didn't make enough noise to bother the adults in the front seat. At first, they talked quietly. Then they started a game of Alphabet Sign.

"'A' on apple sauce," called Sara, reading from a sign advertising applesauce. "B on big."

"'A'!" Because Billy was not yet in school he was not required to tell where he saw the letter.

"'A' on at. 'B' on best." Elaine moved into the lead.

"Elaine," Mother said from the front seat. Keep your voice down."

"'B' on Bartlett, 'C' on California." Now Sara was ahead.

"'B'," called Billy as they passed a sign saying **Los Banos 60 miles**. Elaine thought Billy was at least as loud as she had been, but nobody yelled at him.

And so it went, mile after mile. The trip seemed endless. Even though they were on the main highway between Los Angeles and San Francisco, the road was only a two-lane highway. It went through the center of each little town, and the Wests had to stop at each stoplight. Only between towns did the traffic flow at thirty-five miles an hour, the wartime speed limit. Speeding was illegal. More importantly, since it wasted gasoline, it was seen as unpatriotic. Before they got to Los Banos, the Wests had to pull over onto the shoulder as an Army convoy passed. It was going well over the civilian speed limit. The seventy miles between Fresno and Los Banos took the Wests nearly three and a half hours.

By the time they reached Los Banos, the children had long since tired of the Alphabet Game and were playing "Can You Top This?"

"I saw a dog chasing a cat," said Billy.

"I saw a cat chasing a dog." Elaine answered. "I saw a man riding an elephant."

"I saw six men riding an elephant." said Sara.

"That's two changes, you're only allowed one." Elaine challenged.

"It is only one. I just added the word six."

"But you also changed man to men. That makes two changes."

"But it doesn't count as a change. It's like adding s, ed, ing, a, an, the, and even and. Changing man to men is just like adding an s." Sara spoke with authority.

"No it isn't. It's a different word."

"Girls, you need to quit arguing or play something else." Mother didn't allow fighting, especially between family members.

"Okay," Elaine said. "I'll let it count." She wanted the game to continue.

"I saw a bear riding a tricycle," said Sara.

"I saw a bear eating a tricycle!" Billy giggled at his own joke. They were getting tired and silly. It was not difficult to come up with ever-more-ridiculous "facts."

Los Banos was the halfway point on the journey. It was dusk as they left it and headed toward the pass. By the time they reached Pacheco Pass, it was fully dark. As their father had expected, there was very little traffic, when there was any traffic at all. The light from the moon was bright, making visibility okay, even without normal headlights. Dimmed headlights were required by law on all cars driven after dark on the ocean side of the Coast Range. This tiny blue light was impossible to track from the air, but gave some light on the roadway. Still, it was barely enough to see by. But the treeless hills on the dry side of the Coast Range did little to block the moonlight. They could see the road clearly, and could just make out the oncoming cars by their small, blue lights.

The children tired of "can you top this" and started telling each other stories. This was the part of the trip Elaine liked best. She loved to tell stories and did so anytime she got the chance. She didn't make them up, she just told stories she had heard or read. It always surprised her when anyone thought she'd made the stories up. Elaine had been at it barely fifteen minutes before Billy nodded off to sleep. Sara continued to listen, or at least pretended to listen. Sara knew Elaine loved to tell stories, and she was kind enough to act as though she were listening.

Going west from Los Banos, the next town the Wests passed through was Gilroy. As usual, they could smell Gilroy long before seeing it. Garlic was the chief crop of the area, and it was ripe. Just as the highway came into town, there was a large garlic packing plant. From here, garlic was sent all over the United States. The year before, the packing plant in Gilroy had been brightly lit and busy at night. But that was before Pearl Harbor. This time the packing plant was closed. As they pulled into town, not a single light was visible. Blackouts were occasional drills in Fresno. Here, on the coastal side of the mountains, they were part of the nightly routine. Driving through Gilroy was eerie, like driving through a ghost town. The car crept cautiously though the blackened city. At half past ten, it was still early enough for a few people to be on the streets, but there was no light. Even the traffic lights had been turned off.

Slowly, the car left town and headed for Hecker Pass and the last spur of the Coast Range. Billy was asleep, as was Grandpa, who sat in the middle of the front seat. Elaine turned her face to look out the window, but couldn't see a thing. She cupped her hands to the window, making a little tunnel to shade her eyes and strained through the darkness. Row after row of plum trees lined the road. They were going uphill, higher and higher. Suddenly, even the plum trees were gone. It was almost pitch black, and the road seemed to have disappeared. They had entered the deep shade of a dense redwood forest. Elaine remembered those trees from other years. They grew on both sides of the road, their branches meeting far above, forming a tunnel for the road to go through. The moonlight was gone, blocked by these immense trees. Elaine was beginning to get afraid. The road wound back and forth, the darkness deeper at every turn. It seemed as if there were trees on all sides, even in front of them. Now Elaine was really frightened.

Mother must have been frightened too. "Pull over," Mother ordered, waking Grandpa. "You can't drive in this."

"I can't pull over. There's no shoulder," Father said matter-of-factly.

"Then stop."

"We can't just stop in the middle of the road. We'd probably get hit from behind. We can't turn around either, there's no room and it's too winding to see other cars. We have to go on."

"He's right, Alice," said Grandpa, now fully awake. "His best bet is to go forward."

The car inched forward on the steep, winding highway as Sara and Elaine huddled in fright in the back seat. What had seemed an exciting adventure was now more terrifying than exciting. The road kept winding and winding through the dark. Elaine started to feel sick, but she knew better than to say so.

Father kept apologizing. "I never dreamed it would be this dark! I'll never do this again!"

"Don't worry, dear. We'll make it. You know the road so well."

Elaine heard a slight tremor of fear in Mother's voice. Elaine wanted to cry but clutched Sara's hand instead. Sara took it and squeezed. It was too dark for Elaine to tell if Sara was frightened too. Billy was still sound asleep.

Everyone looked intently ahead. It was as if more people looking for the road would increase the chances of finding it. The car just inched along for what seemed like hours. Then, at last, they were out of the trees and into the moonlight again.

"Oh thank goodness!" said Mother. "I was beginning to think we were going to be in the dark forever."

"That's the longest sixteen miles I've ever driven," sighed Father.

'Had it really only been sixteen miles?' Elaine thought. It had seemed endless.

Close to midnight, they pulled into a blackened Watsonville. They had gone just twenty-two miles since leaving Gilroy over an hour and a half before. The dark city seemed utterly deserted. They crept though the town and turned at the large church silhouetted in the moonlight. The church marked the turn to the Santa Cruz Highway.

After Watsonville, the Wests found themselves once again in open country. The moon was lighting the way again. Feeling safe once more, Elaine and Sara decided Billy definitely had the right idea about how to travel after dark. They were both asleep when, for a short time, the road once again disappeared into the trees.

When Elaine awoke the car was stopped and the air was cool and damp. She could smell the forest.

"We're here," Mother said.

In a sleep-induced stupor, the girls climbed the thirty-seven log-edged dirt steps to the cabin that stood on pilings on the steep hillside. Father carried Billy. Just this once, their parents let the children go to bed in their day clothes. Elaine was fast asleep the minute her head hit the pillow.

CHAPTER 12

July, 1942

Elaine awoke to the sound of birds and the smell of redwoods. The small room was full of the morning sun, but still cold. But then, after the summer heat in Fresno it felt good to feel cold. Sara was already up. The propane-fired stove in the main room warmed Elaine outside while the hot oatmeal warmed her insides. She didn't complain that the milk on the oatmeal was canned and not fresh. She knew there was no refrigerator at the cabin. Through the window, she watched the birds visit the birdfeeder that Grandpa had nailed to a redwood tree next to the porch. The redwoods were so thick that she couldn't see very far in any direction. But she knew where she was going first—to the spring.

As soon as she finished eating, she put on a wool sweater and went outside. She hurried along the path, careful to avoid poison oak by staying on the trail. She passed the huge stumps Sara and she had played house on when they were younger. Sara's house had been on top of the largest stump, Elaine's on one slightly smaller. Both stumps were almost flat on top, and big enough for two little girls and all their dolls. They had visited each other's houses and entertained each other at pretend tea parties on top of those stumps. The ferns gave way to wild sweet peas, blackberry vines, and hazelwood brush in the small clearings where the sun managed to shine through the trees. Elaine hurried to the spring. It was still there—a small, fern-banked stream spilling out of the hillside. Rinsing out the tin cup that sat on a log beside the spring, she filled it with the clear, cool water. It tasted as good as it had last year. Then, rolling up her sleeves, she busied herself in cleaning the streambed of leaves and twigs. Elaine always thought of the spring as hers, and took good care of it.

There was a radio at the cabin, but the radio was so full of static that they rarely turned it on. There were no newspapers. The War seemed long ago and far away. The days settled into a lazy routine of playing, hiking, and wading in the creek into which the stream from the spring flowed. They ate their noon and evening meals on the porch. In the evenings, they pulled the blackout curtains in the main room and played flinch, dominos, or Chinese checkers. Grandmother was much less cross once she was away from Fresno. She didn't seem so particular about her things. She was a very good game player and usually won. Elaine, who very much liked to win, considered losing to Grandmother a small price to pay to stay on her good side.

"Let's go to Santa Cruz tomorrow," Mother suggested one evening while the family was eating dinner. "I need to do some grocery shopping."

"Can we go to the beach when we're there? Please? Please?" begged Billy.

"How about the boardwalk?" pleaded Sara.

"I think we should do both, don't you, John?" Mother always checked with Father. "What with the gas rationing, this will be our only trip into Santa Cruz this year."

"Sure, we'll pack a lunch and make a day of it."

Grandmother chimed in quickly: "We'll just stay here and enjoy the quiet." Elaine's grandparents weren't used to having children around all the time. Elaine wondered if they weren't ready for a quiet day alone.

Next morning, the children gobbled their breakfast. Sara helped Grandmother make the lunch, while Mother organized Billy and Elaine and helped Father pack the car with the beach umbrella, blankets, water jug, swimsuits, towels, and sand toys. When everything was ready, they piled into the car and headed off.

The fog was still hanging over the shore when they got to the beach, so they decided to enjoy the boardwalk until the fog burned off and the sun came out. "Where did all these sailors come from?" Billy exclaimed.

The boardwalk was crowded with sailors. All at once the War was back, but the uniforms were different. Now, instead of the khakis of the Army Air Force, there were the navy blues of the sailors of the Pacific Fleet.

"Probably most of them are from the Alameda Naval Base near San Francisco," said Mother, "they must have come in on the Santa Cruz Special Train from Oakland. It used to run only on weekends to bring day trippers down from San Francisco, but now it's running every day, bringing in sailors."

The planked floor of the boardwalk stretched ahead of them almost endlessly. Elaine could just barely see the Ferris wheel at its far end. On one side of the wide boardwalk were carnival booths, refreshment stands, novelty shops, and amusement rides crowded against one another. On the other side of the raised walk was the sand of the beach. On the seaward side, a wooden railing kept people from falling off into the sand. Beyond the beach lay the fog-shrouded ocean. The sun was just beginning to break through the clouds to do battle with the fog. They all hoped the sun would win and the afternoon would be warm enough to enjoy wading in the ocean. None of the Wests was a strong enough swimmer to actually swim in the wild, tumbling surf.

The smell of the sea mixed with the smell of popcorn and cinnamon as they ambled slowly past a food vendor. They paused at the window of a candy shop to watch the mechanical arms pulling the saltwater taffy. They watched people—mostly sailors—shoot guns at clay pigeons, throw baseballs at silvered milk bottles, throw darts at balloons and play other games. For some of the sailors, Elaine knew, this was a last leave before sailing off to join the battle in the Pacific. As they continued on down the boardwalk, the sun grew ever warmer. A glance at the beach showed that the fog was almost gone. More people were on the beach now. It was going to be a nice afternoon.

"What's that?" asked Billy pointing at a huge, white, football-shaped object that was just coming into view over the horizon.

"That's a blimp," answered Father. "It's used for submarine patrol. See the gondola hanging under it? There are men in there who watch the coast for enemy ships or any sign of a submarine."

"Blimp!" chuckled Billy. "Blimp. Blimp, blimp. How did it get such a funny name?"

"The British wanted a cheap airship and thought one that was limp from not having a solid frame would be the ticket. The A-limp didn't work out, but the B-limp did."

'First the sailors,' Elaine thought, 'and now the blimp;' once again, the War was present.

Soon Elaine heard the roar and screech of the Great Dipper, a roller coaster near the far end of the boardwalk. She could just make out the screams of its passengers above the din of the huge contraption itself. Above and behind Elaine swirled the wooden supports for its tracks. Only Sara was old enough to ride the Great Dipper, but she would rather watch it. Watching the people stagger dizzily from the exit after finishing a ride was a funny sight. Just ahead was the giant Ferris wheel at the end of the boardwalk. The family had planned to ride it, but decided that, what with all the sailors, the line of people was too long. Besides, they were ready for the beach. They hurried back along the boardwalk, stopping only long enough to buy some saltwater taffy for Grandpa.

They left the boardwalk, gathered their things from the car, and found a place on the beach, just above the high tide mark. Father set the beach umbrella up in the sand and spread out a blanket to sit on while Mother got out the lunch. Everyone ate carefully, trying to keep the sand out of the sandwiches. The salt air had made everybody very thirsty. The water from the thermos jug tasted wonderful, even if it wasn't very cold. After lunch, Mother read a book, Father took a nap and the children busied themselves making sand castles while they waited for their lunch to settle so they could go into the water.

When at last that time arrived, Mother and Father held up the beach blanket and a large towel to give the children some privacy, while one at a time Sara, Billy, and Elaine changed into their swimming suits. The adults had outgrown any desire to enter the icy water and elected to watch from the shade of the umbrella. The beach had a lifeguard, but he couldn't be expected to see everything. He kept his eyes on the area where the surf first broke and on the swimmers beyond that line. Sara and Elaine waded out to where the water was almost waist deep. They jumped up as each wave crested. Despite their warnings, Billy tried to follow them. He was tumbled by a wave almost immediately. Sara ran to where he had been standing and got there just in time to see his head pop up from under the water. He was bawling from the cold and from the salt water in his eyes. Sara took him back to Mother, who washed his eyes out with water from the jug. After that, Billy was happy near the shore, where the water seldom reached his ankles. The year before, the children had had inner tubes to ride in the surf, but rubber was too precious now for tire tubes to be used as toys. In and out of the water, they played in the sand and the surf until the wind came up and told their parents it was time to leave.

Back at the cabin Sara, Billy and Elaine took turns rinsing off the sand and salt in the primitive cold water shower in the back yard. The children were all sunburned, especially Billy, whose back was beet red.

Even though she had not wanted to go with them, Grandma was happy to see everybody return. She had brewed some strong tea and let it cool to be ready for treating sunburn when the children got back. While their mother rubbed tea on Billy's reddened skin, Sara and Elaine rubbed it on each other. Although their skin had been exposed to the sun on warm days since spring and was already tanned, it had still burned from the combination of water, beach and sun. The tea took the sting out.

A couple of days later, with their sunburns turned to deeper tans, the spring thoroughly cleaned, and the children tired of playing on the stumps, the vacation came to an end.

Father was careful to time the return trip so that they were well out of the coastal blackout zone before dark, but late enough to miss the heat of the day once they got out of the mountains.

CHAPTER 13

September, 1942

Mother and Elaine were in the kitchen, finishing the breakfast dishes. The sisters took turns helping Mother when there was no school. The kitchen was already hot, despite the open window. Fresno was as hot in September as it was in August or July. It didn't cool off until the rains started in late October.

"I wish school would start," Elaine sighed.

"It will, Elaine," Mother said, "As soon as the grapes are all picked."

"What have the grapes got to do with school?"

"Raisins are our most important crop…"

"I know that! But what does that have to do with school?" Elaine was tired of vacation. She was bored. She wanted to see her friends. Already it was more than a week after Labor Day.

"Don't interrupt, Elaine. Let me finish," Mother said. She spoke softly, but firmly. Mother was patient and understanding, but she did not reward rudeness. "The men are all gone to the War. The ranchers need the school kids to help pick the grapes. School is expected to start once the harvest is over."

Mother got a pitcher of something from the refrigerator.

"What are you doing?" asked Elaine.

"I thought I'd make some ice cream."

Since Elaine had nothing better to do, she stayed to watch Mother. Although the Wests had a refrigerator, many people still had iceboxes. Most people had their milk delivered because iceboxes did not keep milk long. Three mornings a week, the Wests would find three bottles of milk waiting for them on the porch when they got up. The glass bottles were fat with long, narrow necks. The yellowish cream floated in the neck of the bottle, on top of the pale skim milk. To get whole milk Mother shook the bottle. For the last few mornings, instead of shaking the bottle, Mother

Margaret Walters with Mark Walters

had been carefully pouring the cream off the top of the milk and setting it aside. What the family had been drinking and using on their cereal had been mostly skim milk. When she poured off the cream, some of the milk came too. That gave her the light cream the cookbook called for. Now, Mother was using this light cream to make ice cream mix. After the mix was finished, Mother would pour it into two ice cube trays from which she had removed the dividers. The freezing compartment of their refrigerator was only big enough to hold two ice trays. When they made ice cream, of course, they had no ice. But the iceman delivered ice to their neighbors who had iceboxes, or anyone else who wanted to buy some. Whenever Elaine and the other kids saw the ice truck stop in the neighborhood, they would go to the back of the open truck, hoping to find an ice chip to suck on. Once in a while, somebody was successful.

Elaine liked helping Mother. It gave her a chance to talk. She could talk all she wanted to around Mother. Unlike Father, Grandmother, and many other adults, Mother didn't get upset by lots of talking.

"Did you ever help your mother make ice cream?" Elaine asked.

"Yes," Mother said, "We didn't have refrigerators in those days, but sometimes, on special occasions, we bought ice and cranked out a gallon or so of ice cream. You know we had a lot of cows on our farm in Alabama. I remember one time I was helping my mother, your grandmother, separate out the cream. We made a lot of butter from the cream. People there didn't drink much milk. Mostly we fed the skim milk to the pigs. Well, Mother, your grandmother Anna, told me to take a bucketful of skim milk out to the yard and feed it to an orphaned piglet we had. Well, I poured that milk into the pig's trough and that single little piglet drank that whole bucket-full of milk. Then, because it didn't seem possible that one little piglet could drink that whole bucket full of milk, I picked up the piglet and put it into the bucket. That piglet didn't even fill the bucket."

"Where did all the milk the pig drank go?" Elaine's eyes were round with wonder.

"I still haven't figured that out," Mother chuckled.

Elaine never tired of Mother's tales of the farm. Life on a farm was so different from the city life she had always known. She thought she would have liked feeding piglets and milking cows. She particularly would have liked having a horse. She could just imagine it from the movies.

Sara and Elaine were in bed, lights out, waiting for sleep.

"Elaine," Sara said softly so as not to be heard outside the bedroom, as the girls weren't supposed to talk after they went to bed. "Elaine, do you remember Andy, the airman we used to have over for Sunday dinner?

"Of course, he and Bob used to come to dinner a lot. They were going to have dinner with us on my birthday and then Pearl Harbor happened." That whole day was still clear in Elaine's mind.

"Well, I just thought you ought to know"

"Know what?"

"His plane was shot down at Midway."

"Is he okay?"

"No. I mean, probably not. They never found him, Elaine, so he is presumed dead. I mean, the Navy thinks he's dead."

"How do you know?" Elaine was upset by the news, and also upset that Sara knew and she didn't.

"His mother wrote to our parents. She thanked them for giving him all those Sunday dinners."

"Nobody told me," said Elaine, hurt that Mother had informed Sara but not her.

"Nobody told me either," Sara said. "I saw the card and read it. I guess Mother didn't want to upset us."

But Elaine was upset. She had really liked Andy. She wondered how his little sister, the one he had said Elaine reminded him of, felt about the news. She wondered about Bob and the other soldiers they had entertained. Would she ever know what happened to any of them? Would she even know if one of them was killed?

How was dying different from just going away, never to be heard from again?

School finally started in mid-September. It was the first year that the whole school didn't go to the fair. That was because there was no fair. The Japanese who had lived in Fresno county were still at the fairgrounds.

Elaine was happy to get back to school. She always wanted to go as soon as possible, but Mother made her wait, saying the school didn't want the children there early. At twenty minutes to nine the children were at last allowed to leave the house. Across the street and down the sidewalk, Sara, Billy, Rae Dean, Frannie, and Elaine walked on their way to school. Billy was in kindergarten now. He walked to school with the older kids. A sixth grade student patrol officer walked him home at lunchtime. Frannie, who lived down the street, had started to walk with them. Last year Frannie had walked with her older brother, Warren, but now Warren was too old to bother with a little sister. Frannie was a year older than Billy. She was in the first grade. Mother said that Frannie was like a weathervane for trouble. Whenever the children were playing in the backyard, Mother could tell there was trouble when she saw Frannie high-tailing it for home.

"Step on a crack, break your mother's back," called Tommy as he joined the other kids at a run. He, Rae Dean, and Elaine were all in the third grade now.

The other kids immediately began watching their feet.

"I wonder if we'll have an air raid drill today," said Rae Dean, skipping from sidewalk square to sidewalk square, carefully avoiding the cracks.

"Maybe," said Tommy, "we haven't had one for almost two weeks now."

"Oh, I hope we have one soon. I love them," Elaine said wistfully.

"How could anyone love sitting in the dark in the cloak room?" Rae Dean was amazed.

Rae Dean was right, of course. For most kids air raid drills were uncomfortable and boring. But this year Tommy and Elaine's teacher had found a way to make them less so.

"I love air raid drills because in air raid drills it's my job to tell stories to keep the other kids quiet," Elaine explained. "I just love telling stories!"

"She just likes to talk," Sara muttered.

Elaine ignored her and went on, "Besides, I get to keep my head up so I can talk. I've even been practicing a new story."

"You should hear her in bed at night. She lies there talking to herself," Sara said.

"You talk to yourself, Elaine? You must be crazy. Crazy Elaine talks to herself." Tommy laughed.

"Elaine's crazy. She talks to herself." Rae Dean took up the chant.

"It's not so! I'm not crazy!" Elaine put her hands over her ears. She wondered why everyone was making such a fuss. She had talked to herself all of her life. She thought everyone did.

"Insanity runs in families. So my dad says." Tommy was having fun. "Sara must be crazy too, and Billy."

Sara was beginning to wish she'd never said anything in the first place. "Leave us alone. Elaine was only practicing her stories. It's not the same thing as talking to herself. She's not crazy and neither am I."

By now they were in the middle of the next block. They were no longer skipping cracks since now they were curb-walking, arms outstretched for balance, one foot exactly in front of the other.

Then they reached the block that had no sidewalk. By then, several other kids had joined them. The older kids walked the top of the stone retaining wall. The younger children walked below, searching the ground with their eyes.

"There's one." Billy proudly pointed to a heel print in the dirt. On the shoe heel print was a design that looked like the rising sun pictured on the Japanese flag. "I'll bet it's a spy. Anyway, it's the enemy." He kicked out the print. Enemy heel prints had a way of appearing almost anywhere. Who wore such shoes, the kids could only imagine. Even with shoes as scarce as they were, no kid in their school would ever wear shoes whose heels made a print that looked like the Japanese flag.

Tommy and Elaine had always been in the same class. Once you started in a class with a group of kids you stayed with that group from first to sixth grade. "Look," said Tommy not too loudly, "there's that new kid, the one who just started yesterday."

"Do you think his feet are cold?" Tommy pointed to the new boy's bare feet.

Large numbers of people were moving to California. They were coming to take the jobs in the aircraft factories and on the military bases. The newcomers were frequently poor and sometimes barefoot. Grandpa had once said, "Since I was a boy there have been two kinds of people coming to California. One is the shiftless no account kind who take what's easy to get and moves on. The other is the 'Do Better Folks'. They are respectable, hard working poor folks, who come here because they figure that if they work hard and have just a bit of luck they can do better here than they could at home." The new boy's carefully mended clothes, well scrubbed skin, and neatly combed hair marked him as one of the "Do Better Folks." He wouldn't be barefoot for long.

The older kids dropped Billy off at the kindergarten, then walked on to the dusty playground. As they wandered toward the area where their class lined up, Mary Jo joined them.

"Hi, Elaine, Rae Dean. Have you heard the news?" She didn't wait for an answer but went right on. "Patty, you know Patty in our Brownie Troop, she has T. B. Or at least, her father does. They all have to go live at a T.B. sanitarium, her whole family."

Everybody, even children, knew that T.B. was a very serious disease.

"No kidding? Are you sure?"

"Yeah, sure. That way they won't give T.B. to anyone else," Mary Jo insisted. "She lives next door to us. Patty can't even come to school to say goodbye. Patty's mother called us and said I'm supposed to bring Patty's things home. Her folks are already packing. My mother says her father got sick from being a fireman, breathing all that smoke an' all."

"You get T. B. from a germ," Sara corrected.

"Yeah, sure, but it's easier if you're a fireman." Mary Jo tossed her head, making her hair braids fly back and forth.

"How long will they be gone?" Elaine asked.

"No one knows. Weeks, months, years. It all depends on how fast they all get well."

The bell rang and everyone lined up by classes to go inside. Every day at school started the same way. First, the teacher called roll. Every once in a while some boy would say "president" instead of "present", and everyone would laugh and he would lose his recess. Girls never did such a thing. After roll call, there was the flag salute first, and then the children sang "My Country 'tis of Thee." Bonnie, who was new this year, said that in her old school they had sung "God Bless America" instead of "My Country 'tis of Thee" and then the teacher had led them in a prayer afterward. Prayer was not part of the opening exercise in Elaine's school. After that, the students sang the fight songs of the various branches of the military service, in honor of the men who were at war, "fighting to make the world safe for democracy." That morning, Elaine's class started with the anthem of the Field Artillery:

> *"Over hill, over dale,*
> *We will hit the dusty trail;*
> *As those caissons go rolling along..."*

Elaine wondered again what caissons were. It didn't really matter though. Like all the other kids she just loved the song. After the songs were done, the kids settled into their lessons. Certain things were important in school, like sitting up straight, staying in your seat, not talking, waiting until recess to get a drink of water or go to the bathroom, and never asking your teacher for permission to sharpen your pencil until it was too dull to make any mark at all. Teachers believed that students needed to practice all of these things in order to learn properly.

Elaine had always liked school, but she couldn't begin to tell anyone why. It was mostly being there, with the other kids, doing what kids did.

Much of school was boring. Everyone in the class had the same assignment and had the same amount of time in which to do it. If Elaine worked at her normal speed, she always finished way ahead of most of the others. If the teacher knew she was finished, she would insist that Elaine check her work for errors, and then check it again. Elaine saw no sense in doing anything more than once, so she became quite expert at doing things that kept her from finishing early. The trick was to stretch the assignment out by doing something else on the side. Of course there was always the chance of getting caught playing tick-tack-toe, secretly reading, or drawing. But the risk was not great, because the teacher seldom left the front of the room. Since anyone could remember, students had been seated at school alphabetically by last names, and Elaine sat in the back because her last name began with a "w." Besides that, Elaine had a good reputation, and it wouldn't occur to the teacher that she would do anything more serious than visit with a neighbor.

Elaine spent a lot of time at school daydreaming. Today, she was thinking over the fun everyone in the neighborhood had had the last weekend, turning a vacant lot in the middle of the block into a community garden. Almost everyone on the block had turned out to prepare the soil.

The children hadn't been crazy about the idea; they would have preferred that the lot stay empty, the way it was before. The weeds in the lot had never been mowed and were taller than Billy's head. The neighborhood children would tramp the grass down into "rooms" and "streets" and play in it for hours. It was great for hide and seek, too. Even the tall kids could disappear, if they crouched down. The lot worked equally well for playing "cowboys and Indians." But everyone had to make sacrifices in wartime and the kids understood that giving up their play space for food growing was necessary. In addition to her own people, the United States was feeding Britain and most of the other allied fighting forces as well. As a nation, the United States needed to grow more food. Transporting the food was also a problem. The trains that in normal times carried food from one part of the country to another were now overloaded with military supplies. The government had asked that people grow as much of their own food as they could. Vegetable gardens were now called victory gardens.

The man who owned the lot had given the neighbors permission to plant vegetables in it, and so that weekend the grown-ups had gone out to it with hoes, picks, and shovels and prepared the soil for planting. It had taken them almost all day, from sunup to sundown, and now the lot looked nothing like it had before. Where there had been weeds, now there were neatly furrowed rows. Next Saturday, people were going to plant the seeds of those vegetables that could be planted in the fall.

Those who could started raising their own meat as well. In fact, Father had decided that the family would start keeping rabbits for that purpose. For the past week, he had busied himself in the evenings, building rabbit hutches in the backyard.

"Elaine!" The teacher's voice called her back to the present. "Please pay attention. This is important! You all need to be able to tell an enemy plane from an American one. Boys and girls, who can tell me what plane this is?" Using her long, wooden pointer, the teacher pointed to one of the pictures on the narrow corkboard over the front black board. The pictures were all of airplanes, Japanese and American. It was taken for granted that no German planes would reach the West Coast. The planes were shown from all angles: diving, rolling on one side, flying straight and level, and so forth.

Hands shot into the air. It was no surprise to Elaine that almost all of them belonged to boys. Elaine was not very good at airplane identification. Nor was she very interested in it. Her mind wandered off again, but she made sure to keep her eyes fixed on the airplane pictures. She was thinking about what she was going to be for Halloween this year.

CHAPTER 14

October, 1942

Elaine was playing jacks in her corner one Friday evening when Father came home from work and started talking to Mother. Elaine liked listening to adults talking to each other. Listening from her corner, she felt like a secret agent gathering information.

"Well, Alice, they've started moving the Japanese out of the fairgrounds."

"It's about time! I don't know how those poor people have stood being there this long. Where are they going?"

"To temporary camps until the end of the War. "

"Where?"

"I don't know. I just saw them being loaded unto Army trucks."

"I hope it's better than where they are."

"I'm sure it is. Why else would they move them? How much time 'till dinner?"

"About an hour."

"Good. That's about the time it will take for me to finish the last rabbit hutch."

Elaine parked her jacks' ball and rushed to find Sara. Sara was in the backyard with Billy.

"Daddy is finishing the rabbit hutches this evening. I can hardly wait to get the rabbits."

"I wonder what they'll look like. Remember at the fair the year before last? The rabbits came in all different colors," said Sara.

"I hope mine looks like Thumper," Billy said. The movie, "Bambi", had just come out. Playing "Bambi" was very popular in the neighborhood, each kid pretending to be a different animal in the movie. Billy always wanted to be Thumper. The children played on the swings as they watched Father finish the rabbit hutches.

The next morning, after breakfast, Father said, "As soon as you girls finish helping your mother with the dishes, we'll take the car to get the rabbits." It didn't take them long. Car trips were rare, and this one had an exciting destination. While Billy, Sara, and Elaine climbed into the back seat of the car, Father loaded a cardboard box into the trunk.

"Elaine, you sit in the middle," reminded Mother.

"Do I have to?" she pleaded.

"Yes, it's quite a ways and you know Billy and Sara sometimes quarrel when they sit next to each other."

"What's the box for?" Billy quietly asked.

"It's probably for bringing the rabbits home in," Elaine reasoned, seeing no other possibility.

"How many rabbits are we going to get?"

"One apiece, at least. We each get our own doe, remember."

Mother had explained it all to them the previous Saturday when the children had asked her what their father was building in the backyard. They had asked him first, but he'd said, "I'm busy. Go ask your mother."

Mother had explained, "The family was going to go into the rabbit raising business. Each of you will get your own doe--that's what you call a mother rabbit, a doe. You can name her whatever you like. You can make a pet of her if you want to. There will also be a buck, or daddy rabbit, and two other does belonging to the family. Your father is making the rabbit hutches in the back yard. That's where the rabbits will live.

"The bunnies your doe has will be yours, but you are not to make pets out of them. When they are old enough, they will be killed.

"But what if we don't want them killed," asked Sara

"You will have no choice. We can't keep them all. The Army Air Corps needs the hides. We'll sell the hides, and that will pay for the expense of feeding and otherwise caring for the rabbits. That money will belong to the family. The sale of the meat from the rabbits produced by your doe will be your profit. Each of you will be expected to take turns watering and feeding the rabbits and helping your father clean the hutches." She went on to explain the whole plan in more detail.

In the car Elaine continued to explain the plan to Billy. "We get to name our doe and everything. She's ours and her babies are ours," Elaine said.

She knew her little brother was too young to understand everything the first time he was told. "Only we're not to make pets of the babies 'cause when they get big enough they have to be killed."

"Why do they have to be killed?" asked Billy.

"For their fur. The Air Corps needs the fur to line flight jackets." Then, seeing the puzzled look on Billy's face, she continued, "There's no heat in a B-17. They fly very high, and the higher they fly, the colder it gets."

"How come?" Billy asked.

This seemed illogical to Elaine too, since the closer you got to the sun, the hotter it should be. But then, she knew from experience that it was cooler in the mountains than in the valley, so it must be so.

Ignoring her brother's question, she went on. "Anyway, the flight jackets have to keep the pilot and crew warm, so they're lined with rabbit fur, 'cause it's so warm. Growing rabbits will be our contribution to the war effort. Besides, rabbits are good eating and there is a meat shortage."

By now the family was just beyond the outskirts of Fresno. Finally, they turned into a dusty drive beside a house whose age could be determined more by the large trees that shaded it than by the house itself. The Fresno summers were so hot, one of the first things any builder did was to plant shade trees. Trees didn't grow there naturally, except along the river. As they got out of the car, the rabbit rancher, who had been expecting them, came out of the house and shook hands with Father.

"Good to see you again, John."

"Good to see you, too, Tom. I'd like you to meet my wife, Alice. And these runabouts are Sara, Elaine, and Billy. We've come to take some of your rabbits off your hands."

"Now's the perfect time of year for it, not too hot or too cold."

Father took the cardboard box out of the trunk.

"The rabbits are this way," said Tom. The adults walked ahead while the children followed them down the dirt path toward a long, open sided shed located behind the house. Elaine edged ahead, trying to hear what they were saying. Billy and Sara were content to trail along behind.

"The shed gives the rabbits some shade. With that heavy coat they will die if they get too hot," Tom was saying.

"We have a large walnut tree in our yard," said Father. "The hutches will go under that, behind a small fence to keep the neighborhood dogs from bothering them."

"That should be enough shade for 'em. A good doe will litter five-six times a year," the rancher continued. "Average litter is eight to ten."

The rabbits were in a long, wide shed. It was not really a building, just a roof with a concrete floor. Rabbit hutches stood one on top of another, row after row. Each hutch was made mostly of wire mesh fastened to a wooden frame. The rest of the hutch was wood. The floor was also of mesh, allowing the rabbit droppings to fall through to a tray below. The tray could be removed like a drawer for easy cleaning. In the hutches, white rabbits of various sizes were eating, drinking, or just lying around. Some of the younger ones were even playing.

"It's important not to disturb a doe when she litters," the rancher said. He lifted the roof off one of the hutches and showed us the nesting box behind the open area. Its sides and floor were entirely of wood. The floor of the nesting box was covered with wood shavings. In the nesting box, a doe and her young would be out of sight unless someone lifted the roof. The doe could come and go into and out of the nesting area through a hole. In most of the hutches the doe was in plain sight, in some the rabbit was in the nesting area looking out through the hole, in others she was totally out of sight. Father had obviously seen these hutches before, as the ones in the back yard were exact copies.

"Here they are. These have been weaned about a week now. Within a couple of months they'll be good breeders."

The family stopped in front of one of the hutches. Inside, a dozen or so bunnies, about the size of small kittens, were playing.

"Oh! They're so cute!" the kids exclaimed almost together.

"Look at the pink eyes," said Sara.

"They're all white," said Billy, "Thumper wasn't all white."

"Their fur is white. The inside of their ears, even their noses are pink," Elaine observed.

"Each of you, pick one out," said Father "and we'll see if it's female."

Billy pointed to an active bunny that looked like it might someday thump its foot. The rancher caught it, turned it over, examined it carefully and handed it to Billy.

"Here you are, Sonny. Handle her gently. Keep your hand under her feet. Hold her up against your chest. Careful, don't squeeze her. That's right."

Billy was delighted with his Thumper. He began to sooth her fur.

"He's so soft," he said almost in a whisper.

"He's a she," Sara corrected. But Billy wasn't listening. He was talking to Thumper. Sara pointed to a rabbit, but after close observation, Tom, the rabbit rancher, declared it a male and put it back. Her second pick was female. She named her doe Snowball.

It took three tries for Elaine to choose a female, but at last the rancher handed her a bunny. "I'm going to call you Lucky, 'cause you're Lucky to be my rabbit instead of part of some pilot's flight jacket," she cooed into the bunny's tiny pink ear.

Mother took the rabbits one by one and tied a piece of colored ribbon around each little doe's neck before placing each one in the cardboard box. "Billy, Thumper has the blue ribbon. Elaine, Lucky has the green. Sara, Snowball's ribbon is red. Can you all remember that?"

Father picked out three more rabbits-- two more females, and a young male from an entirely different litter.

On the way home in the car, the rabbits safely tucked away in the cardboard box, Elaine thought about what Mother had said about the rabbit business. Elaine thought it would be fun feeding and watering the rabbits. She was not so sure about cleaning the hutches.

Mother had told the children that Mr. Sanders, the butcher, was willing to pay 19 cents a pound for a dressed rabbit ready to be fried. A rabbit fryer was about three to three and a half pounds, which meant that the meat of each grown rabbit would be worth a dollar and sixty cents. Elaine busily tried to figure out how much money she would make from in the rabbit business. A dollar-sixty would buy sixteen double scoop ice cream cones or pay her way into eight Saturday afternoon matinees at the Tower Theater. The rabbit rancher had said that she could expect eight bunnies in each litter. Elaine had not yet learned her times tables beyond two, but since she had always spent a lot of time playing Monopoly, she knew her fifteens at least until 5 X 15 because Illinois Ave. was her favorite piece of property, and it took $150 to buy a house for Illinois Ave. Four fifteens made sixty, and eight was twice that, or one hundred twenty. One litter would give her at least twelve whole dollars. But the rabbit rancher had also said to expect five litters a year. She didn't know how much five times twelve was, but it sounded like a lot. It seemed to her that she would be rich!

CHAPTER 15

November, 1942

Saturday before Thanksgiving, Father came home with a live turkey. Mother had started planning the Thanksgiving dinner well in advance. She had tried to order a turkey from the butcher, as she always did, despite the fact it would use up many precious ration stamps. The butcher, however, could not guarantee he could get dressed turkeys, even for Thanksgiving. Father made sure there would be a Thanksgiving turkey by buying a live one, straight from a turkey rancher at the Farmer's Market. He made quite a sight, wheeling the turkey home on the back of his bicycle. And because the government didn't ration livestock, he had also saved ration stamps. Sara, Billy, and Elaine named the turkey Tom, Tom Turkey. Tom was confined to the small, fenced area of the back yard where the rabbit hutches were. Father tied a cord around Tom's leg and attached the other end to a good-sized rock. This kept Tom from becoming airborne or flapping himself over the low fence.

Each day, the children fed him chicken meal and table scraps. Despite Mother's caution not to get too friendly with something the family planned to eat, the children tried to make a pet out of Tom. He would have none of it. Every time anyone got close to him he attacked. One time Sara got too close and Tom pecked her legs so hard she had great red welts for days. He was a nasty tempered bird—a real turkey! After Sara got pecked, the children were afraid to go into the rabbit yard to feed the rabbits. Mother, who was not going to be intimidated by a mere turkey, took over their job until Thanksgiving.

The Sunday before Thanksgiving, as Elaine sat in church not listening to the sermon, she counted the stars on the banner hanging on the church wall. The banner was royal blue silk, trimmed with a gold edge. There was a silver star on the banner for each member of the church who was serving in the military. There was a gold star for each serviceman who had died. Elaine counted thirty-seven silver stars and three gold ones. But she knew that some of the silver stars should have been gold because some of the silver stars stood for National Guardsmen missing in the Philippines. No one knew what had happened to these men after the Philippines fell to the Japanese. One of the gold stars represented Jimmy Clark. He was just barely eighteen when he died at Guadalcanal. His youngest sister, Cindy, was in Elaine's Sunday school class. Cindy cried so much the one time Elaine had asked about him that Elaine never mentioned him again.

There were posters up all over town now, warning people not to talk about the war. The posters said enemy spies might be listening. But, Elaine didn't like to talk about the war anyway, because too often when she did people got upset. Looking around the congregation now, she did not see any man younger than her father who was not in uniform. Elaine looked back at the banner and wondered: would there be more gold stars now that the American Army had started fighting the Germans in North Africa?

The day before Thanksgiving, Father went outside, got an ax from the garage, and chopped off Tom Turkey's head. No one was at all upset. The girls helped Mother prepare the bird. First Mother held the whole bird by the feet and dipped the rest of it into boiling water to loosen the feathers. Mother carefully removed and set aside the long tail feathers. Later, she would wash them, so the kids could play with them. Mother then handed the bird to Sara and Elaine with instructions on how to remove the rest of the feathers. Sara and Elaine worked at the small table, pulling out the smelly feathers by the handful and throwing them away. When they had finished pulling out all the feathers they could get, Mother singed off the rest by carefully holding the turkey over the gas burner on the stove. She slowly rotated it as the tiny pinfeathers burned away. The few broken quills that were left, Mother plucked out with tweezers. Once the skin was clear and clean, she cut off the feet. She then opened the abdominal cavity with a sharp knife and removed the organs. The liver, heart, and gizzard she saved for the gravy; the rest of the innards she threw away. Now the bird was ready for cooking.

The next morning the girls helped Mother stuff the turkey and put it into the oven, while Billy helped Father get the table ready. Father put the leaves in the dining room table and set it lengthwise, half in the living room, half in the dining room. He then put the kitchen table on one end and two card tables on the other end. Billy helped him pad the tables with clean folded sheets. They used three tablecloths to turn four tables into one very long table with somewhat uneven sides. The girls and Billy used both the Sunday and the everyday china to set the table for eighteen. Mother advised where to put the place cards the children had made in the shape of pilgrim hats. That way, each person would know where to sit. Father rounded up the chairs. There were only fourteen chairs, but the piano bench could seat two children, and Mother's vanity bench another child. As the youngest, Billy could sit on the kitchen stool, and for once be as tall as anybody.

Ethel, one of Mother's younger sisters, arrived early to help Mother with the cooking. Just this year Ethel had started teaching cooking at Bakersfield High School. Soon, Grandma and Grandpa West arrived. They brought fresh carrots and late green beans from their garden and some olives from their tree. The olives had been treated with lye to remove the bitterness and then put into salt water to cure for almost a year. Uncle Clifford, Aunt Ellen, and their daughter, Gladys, arrived next with the pies. Gladys was about the same age as Sara, but she was a little different. No one ever said what exactly was wrong with Gladys, but she rarely talked and didn't like to play the same games that the other children did. She just scribbled in coloring books, and had not yet learned to read. Sara and Elaine were always glad to see her at family gatherings, because she actually liked to wash dishes.

Mother's youngest sister, Pearl, with her fiancé, Earl, were the next to arrive. He was a large, ever-cheerful soldier from Arkansas. They had met at church. He was in the Army, but could not serve overseas because of a bad tear gland. A tiny tear would periodically roll down his cheek. This moisture made it impossible for a gas mask to get a tight seal against his face. Poison gas had not been used since World War I, but it had done such terrible damage to men on both sides in that war that it was still greatly feared in combat zones. Since he was unable to be in combat, Earl was stationed at a nearby signal corps base. Although it was miles from any tree, the base was called Camp Pine Dale. Edward and Nathan, two servicemen who had been the Wests' most recent Sunday guests, walked up from the bus stop to join the family for the holiday as well. Everyone hoped it would make the airmen less lonely for their own families at Thanksgiving.

While the other guests settled into the living room chairs to talk, Mother and her sisters disappeared into the kitchen to finish the dinner.

Elaine followed them. She liked to listen to them talk. Pearl chatted merrily about Earl. Soon the conversation turned to the stories of Thanksgivings past, when Mother and her sisters had been children on the farm. They talked of work, accidents, pranks, and parties. Elaine was surprised to hear that their parties included dancing, since she knew that her father's parents considered dancing a sin. Elaine loved these stories. She tried to imagine Mother as a child. She tried to picture Mother's mother, Grandmother De Vore, who had died shortly before Sara was born. Elaine knew little about her. Grandmother De Vore had been unwell, but she was cheerful, played the piano, loved people, and hosted parties. Elaine was sure that, had she lived, Grandmother De Vore would have been the loving grandmother Elaine had always wanted.

The kitchen was hot and Elaine was in the way, so Mother suggested that she go outside. Billy and Sara were already in the yard and had gotten their does out of the rabbit yard to show Gladys. Elaine went and got Lucky. Lucky was mostly grown now, and it was good to hold her again. Elaine had not been able to pet her while Tom was in the rabbit yard. She carried Lucky to the area of the lawn that had the most clover. Thumper and Snowball were already there, munching on the clover under the watchful eyes of Billy and Sara. The rabbits liked to be out of their hutches. The smell of baking bread and roasting turkey drifted out of the slightly opened kitchen window. The kids let the rabbits graze a bit, then put them back into their hutches and started jumping rope. Gladys was really good at jumping rope. She seemed to never miss. Sara and Elaine got very tired of turning the rope for her.

At last Father called them in to wash up for dinner. Once everyone was seated, Grandpa West led a prayer of Thanksgiving. His voice quivered with emotion as he thanked God for the many blessings He had given them. He asked God to protect those at the table and their loved ones far away. He prayed for an end to the war and the safe return of the boys from overseas. His prayer made Elaine think about how far Edward and Nathan were from home, and about the danger they would soon be facing. She saw in her mind the banner of stars hanging on the wall of the church. She thought about how sad Andy's parents and the Clarks must be this Thanksgiving knowing that their sons would never come home. She knew how truly fortunate her family was.

Soon after Thanksgiving, Elaine was sick again. She had been sick a lot that fall. She had almost constant colds, coughs, sore throats, and stomach upsets. Her parents decided it was time to take her to the doctor. Since it was not an emergency, the earliest appointment they could get was at the end of January. There was a shortage of doctors. Many doctors, the Wests' family doctor among them, had volunteered to serve in the military. Other doctors had been drafted. Only the doctors judged too old or physically unfit for military service were left at home.

The first anniversary of Pearl Harbor—Elaine's eighth birthday--came and went. Elaine still resented the fact that the Japanese had chosen her birthday, of all days, to attack the US. It meant that she could no longer expect her birthday to be happy and cheerful.

Christmas came a little over two weeks later. It was still merry, but for many, the gaiety was clouded because their loved ones were far away. Inside every store and most houses there were brightly colored and lighted decorations. Outside, there were also brightly colored decorations, but no lights at all. Music was everywhere, especially at night, as if to make up for the absence of outside lighting.

There would be servicemen at Christmas dinner, but the Christmas Eve celebration was just for the family. That was when they exchanged gifts. Elaine received a new navy blue wool coat made by Grandmother West, and a large bottle of toilet water. Elaine thought was an odd name for such sweet smelling stuff. She also got some paper dolls and some lovely stationery. None of the children had expected toys, not even five-year-old Billy. Everyone knew that the factories were needed for making more important things. Even Santa's elves were no longer making toys.

There were almost as many people at Christmas dinner as there had been at Thanksgiving. There was no ham or roast beef, but Grandpa West had raided his chicken house so the whole family could enjoy a feast of fried chicken. After the dinner dishes were done, everyone gathered around the piano while Earl played and sang. Earl had never had a lesson and couldn't read a note, but he could play any tune he had ever heard. There was a rollicking, joyful sound to his playing and singing. After the family had sung all the Christmas carols they knew, Earl took requests. Everyone had a favorite: "A Froggie Would A'Courting Go", "Big Rock Candy Mountain", "Billy Boy", "Cindy", "Home on the Range", and on and on. The family sang with Earl when they knew the words and just listened when they didn't. It was a very joyous afternoon. Even the airmen, who were miles from home and days from live combat, seemed to genuinely enjoy themselves.

1943 dawned without lights or sparks. The blackout was still in force, and explosives were too badly needed for war to be wasted on fireworks. Instead, at midnight people honked their car horns and shouted and sang. Everyone hoped the war would not last too many more years.

CHAPTER 16

January, 1943

Elaine's appointment with the doctor was set for late January. Elaine just kept getting sick, even through the holidays, so Mother kept her home from school a lot that winter. She also put her to bed early every night so she could get extra sleep. Getting extra sleep was easier said than done because lying there in the dark Elaine kept thinking about all the terrible illnesses she might have. Maybe she had TB. Lots of people got that. Or scarlet fever like Carol Ann, a girl in her scout troop, whose hair had all come out from the fever. And then there was Mabel. Mabel was two years older than everyone else in the class because she had spent two years home in bed with rheumatic fever. Elaine sure didn't want to spend two years in bed; going to bed early was bad enough.

But what could it be that was making her so sick? After all, she had already had all the common childhood illnesses. She could remember the two-week measles, when she had to stay in bed in a darkened room for what seemed like forever. She had also had the three-day measles but she couldn't remember them. She and Billy had had the chicken pox at the same time. Her case of the mumps had been very light, not anything like the painful, mouth puckering illness her friends talked about. And then, Mother still talked about the time when only four months old, Elaine had had the whooping cough. Elaine couldn't remember it, of course, but Mother had told her that she had coughed so violently that she would turn red and even purple. Mother had been greatly afraid she would lose her baby girl. Thousands of babies died from the disease each year. By the time Billy was born, there was a vaccine for whooping cough, as well as that other childhood killer, diphtheria. Mother made sure Billy got the vaccine.

But even Mother didn't know what was the matter with Elaine this time. She did not know what caused the violent bouts of vomiting. She made Elaine stay in the house a lot. It seemed like every time Elaine went outside she got sick. At school Elaine spent a lot of recesses lying down on one of the beds in the nurse's office.

Both Mother and Elaine were glad when it was finally time for the long-awaited appointment with the doctor. They walked two blocks to the bus stop and waited on the bench for the bus. Like everyone else, they went almost everywhere on the bus now, or they walked. Like always, the bus was crowded when it came. Fifteen minutes later they got off the bus and walked around the corner a short distance to a very large white house with white columns supporting the roof of a large porch. Out on the front yard was a sign that read, "Dr. Hirsch, MD. Eye, Ear, Nose, & Throat." They walked into a huge front room that looked like the parlor of a large house. As they waited for the doctor, Mother and Elaine sat on the sofa and admired the pictures on the wall. The seascapes reminded Elaine of Santa Cruz. She wondered if the doctor lived in the rest of the house. Dr. Hirsch turned out to be much older than their regular doctor, Dr. James, who had delivered Sara, Elaine, and Billy. Dr. James had even come to their house whenever anyone was very ill. Dr. Hirsch listened to Mother tell about Elaine's health problems, about how Elaine would vomit for hours, unable to keep anything down, all the while running a high fever. She mentioned how worried she was that, skinny as Elaine already was, she seemed to be losing weight.

He took out his stethoscope and put it on Elaine's bare chest. The stethoscope was cold. She squirmed.

"Sit still!" he scolded, as he listened to her heart and lungs. Then he stuck a thermometer in her mouth while he took her pulse. Then he removed the thermometer and put a stick in Elaine's mouth. Holding down her tongue, he looked down her throat. "Say ahhhh."

"Ahhhh."

He pressed down farther back and shown a light down Elaine's throat. "Again, Ahhh."

"Ahhh," Elaine gagged.

Dr. Hirsch turned to Mother. He talked to her as if Elaine wasn't even in the room. "Her tonsils are infected. They are poisoning her entire system. They need to come out, but she needs to be stronger and healthier first." He sighed and continued, "I wish you'd come in sooner. We really don't have any medicine for fighting a bacterial infection once it gets into the body."

"What about penicillin?" Mother asked.

Dr. Hirsch seemed surprised. "Where did you hear about penicillin?"

"Oh, I don't know. I read about it somewhere."

"Humph, it's unusual to have a patient so well informed about medicines. But since you do know about penicillin, I'll tell you that it is unlikely that we will be able to use penicillin for civilians until after the war is over. For now, penicillin is too difficult to make in quantity. There is only a tiny amount of it at any one time and so it is restricted to life and death situations in military hospitals, where it can be distilled from the soldiers' urine and used again.?

'That's all that was wrong with me,' Elaine thought, 'infected tonsils.' It was a big relief. Just about everyone she knew had already had his or her tonsils out.

"As for this little lady," Dr. Hirsch continued. "For now she needs to eat lots of good food whether she is hungry or not. Put some more meat on her bones, Mrs. West. A tablespoon full of Vitamin B complex will help her appetite and build her strength. I assume you already give her a daily spoonful of cod liver oil." He looked sternly at Mother.

"Yes, of course, ever since she was a baby."

"Be sure she gets plenty of bed rest to build up her strength. Put her to bed at 7:00, 7:30 at the latest. And dress her warmly. I'll write her a note she can take to school so that they will let her wear pants instead of skirts. She needs to keep her legs covered. Hopefully, she'll be strong enough for the operation by the time school is out."

Elaine was not happy with Dr. Hirsch's prescription. How could she eat more? As it was, she was rarely hungry enough to finish her supper. Food just didn't taste good. There always seemed to be a bad taste in her mouth, and her nose was always stuffed up. And, although she did not like feeling cold most of the time, she was not looking forward to being the only girl in the school dressed in pants instead of a skirt. And going to bed early! It seemed to her that she already went to bed earlier than any of her friends. Now her bedtime was being moved up an hour. Between the war and her tonsils, it was going to be a long winter.

As it turned out though, Dr. Hirsch's prescription was not as unpleasant as Elaine had expected. Grandmother made Elaine three pairs of corduroy pants using the same pattern she used when she made pajamas. The kids at school quickly got used to seeing her in pants. It was nice not being called "Toothpicks" anymore, since in slacks no one could see her skinny legs. She certainly didn't miss feeling cold and shivery all the time. As for the food, she had expected more vegetables since Mother was always insisting that the children eat them, but instead Elaine got more treats. After school, Mother made her homemade milk shakes using milk, vanilla, sugar, and raw egg, or bowls of chocolate pudding, tapioca or junket, and all the homemade cookies she would eat. Still, Elaine had to eat dinner as usual. Mother put extra large amounts of butter on all her food, even though it was expensive and tightly rationed. Elaine liked butter, but cleaning her plate at every meal was a real chore. Besides, she thought having to clean her plate was unfair, since she had no say about what or how much food was put there. Father scolded her for picking at her food so often that Sara began to eat very slowly herself, so Father would not accuse Elaine of holding up the whole meal.

The worst part of Dr. Hirsch's prescription was the continuing extra bed rest. It changed the entire family routine. Dinner was always exactly at six o'clock. Sara and Elaine were still responsible for doing the dishes, alternating the washing and the drying duties. But now, instead of having after dinner play time, story time came right after the dinner dishes were done. The girls would sit on the couch, one on each side of Mother. Billy would sit on her lap as Mother read. First she would read a short Bible story for Billy, then from the Bible itself. After that she read from a children's classic. She read *Heidi*, *Peter Pan*, the Oz books, *Alice in Wonderland*, *Dr. Doolittle*, and just about every other well-know children's story. The children loved this nightly ritual. Father was always in the living room during story time. He held an adult book in his hands, but he so rarely turned the pages, Elaine suspected that he, too, was listening to Mother read. Immediately following the reading, Mother sent Elaine to brush her teeth, wash, and go to bed. Even Billy got to stay up a bit longer! It just wasn't fair!

Elaine was never sleepy so early in the evening. Even in winter, when it was dark outside, sleep did not come easily. She resented that she was not even allowed to read, but Mother insisted that the light be off. To pass the time Elaine would lie in bed practicing for the air raid drills at school by telling stories out loud to herself. If sleep still didn't come, she would set herself math problems she could solve in her head. Some nights, lying alone in the dark, she would count by sevens beginning with four and then check herself by doing it backwards. Other nights, she would start with a small number, double it, double that, and so forth. Eventually, she would fall asleep.

Weeks turned into months and, as Elaine began to feel better, she wanted a normal bedtime. Finally, in mid-May, Dr. Hirsch agreed that she was stronger and said that she could stay up half an hour longer. He would take her tonsils out as soon as school was over.

CHAPTER 17

June, 1943

At last school was out. The time for the long-awaited tonsillectomy was here. However, Fresno's hospitals were full of servicemen who'd been wounded in the Pacific. With so many seriously injured men to care for, hospital beds and operating rooms could not be spared for simple procedures like tonsillectomies. For Elaine, the doctor's office would have to do.

Even that turned out to be a problem, because the day before the surgery was scheduled, the car would not start. Father figured it might be the fuel pump, so he took it off and bicycled down to the auto garage. The mechanic agreed it was the fuel pump, but he didn't have another one. Car parts were in such short supply that he would have to rebuild the fuel pump. There was no way he could get it done in time.

"We'll just have to take the bus," Mother said. "It's a short ride. The bus stop is very near the doctor's office. We'll be fine."

"Getting there is one thing," said Father, "but getting home with a sick child is another."

"I've got it all worked out. Dorothy will be babysitting Sara and Billy. They can all meet us at the bus stop with Billy's red coaster wagon. We can wheel Elaine home in that so that she won't have to walk."

It all sounded like an exciting adventure to Elaine. Getting her tonsils out was an expected part of childhood, a sort of shared experience. Her friends had told her all about it, and said that after they got their tonsils out they could not eat anything but Popsicles, ice cream, pudding, and Jell-O for days. She loved all four. In fact, she loved anything sweet and looked forward to feasting on desserts.

The next morning, Elaine dressed quickly and hurried to breakfast.

"No breakfast for you this morning, Elaine, remember?" said Mother. "The doctor prefers that you have an empty stomach."

Elaine waited in the living room while the rest of the family ate. After breakfast, Father left for work on his bicycle. Sara and Billy went out to play.

"The children's lunch is in the refrigerator, as is yours," Mother instructed Dorothy as soon as she arrived. "After lunch the children are to rest and read for half an hour. After that, they can play. If the temperature is over ninety degrees, they can play in the water outside if they want to. No snacks before lunch or after four o'clock. When Elaine and I are ready to start home, probably around four thirty, I'll telephone. Take the red coaster wagon, the one with pillows in it that's out by the back steps, and walk down to the bus stop with Sara and Billy and wait for us. If you need to talk to me before then, I'll be at this number." She pointed at a number written on the piece of paper that she'd tacked on the small corkboard by the telephone.

Elaine waited eagerly on the couch, her eyes moving from Mother to the clock to Mother again. Mother darted to and fro, taking care of last minute details. Finally, she said, "Come on, Elaine; let's walk on down to the bus stop."

"Goodbye," called Billy and Sara as Mother and Elaine left through the back yard.

They walked the two blocks to the bus stop in no time at all. Mother carried a shopping bag. In it were Elaine's pajamas, a lightweight blanket, and a book for Mother to read while she waited. The wait at the bus stop was short. Although the day promised to be hot, the morning was cool and pleasant. When the bus pulled up to the bus stop, it was already full of people, mostly men and women on their way to work. Everyone who could rode the bus to work to save his or her gasoline ration. When Elaine and Mother boarded, one of the men stood to give Mother a seat. Elaine stood in the aisle near her. The ride was short. They got off and walked a short distance to Dr. Hirsch's house. They waited only a few minutes in the waiting room. Soon, the nurse came and led them into another room, where she took Elaine's temperature and checked her pulse. The nurse asked Elaine to put on her pajamas and hop up onto the examining table. She explained that same table would be used as an operating table. Dr. Hirsch came in minutes later and examined Elaine's throat. Then he told her to lie down on the table. He signaled to the nurse, and she held a smelly piece of gauze over Elaine's nose and told her to count backwards from ten. She only made it to seven before she fell asleep.

When Elaine awoke, she was lying in bed in a small bedroom. Mother was sitting in a rocking chair next to the bed, reading a book. Elaine's throat hurt. She was very thirsty. She tried to talk but little sound came out.

"Don't talk, dear," said Mother. "I'll get the nurse." She left the room and returned shortly.

The nurse arrived with a Popsicle. "I'll bet you're thirsty," said the nurse. "Here, suck on this."

The melted ice felt good on her throat. Her stomach began to lose its queasy feeling. After the second Popsicle, she began to feel stronger, more awake.

About half an hour later Dr. Hirsch came in. He looked Elaine over carefully, felt her pulse, listened to her heart, and decided she was ready to leave. Mother and the nurse wrapped her in the light blanket. Then they helped her out to the bench at the bus stop. The nurse promised to call Dorothy and tell her they were on their way. The wait for the bus seemed long to Elaine. She kept dozing off. When the bus finally came, it was standing room only. However, the people in the front seat immediately went to the rear to make room for the woman with the sick child. Elaine rode home, cuddled in Mother's arms. Elaine felt very weak and years younger than she had been that morning. The ride seemed very long.

Dorothy, Billy, and Sara were waiting at the bus stop with Billy's little red wagon, all lined with pillows. Mother helped Elaine get comfortable in the wagon. Dorothy pulled her home while Billy and Sara walked beside the wagon, giving Elaine words of sympathy and encouragement. As they pulled her home, Elaine could hear the scratch of the wagon's wheels on the concrete and feel each crack. When they got home, Mother helped her get into bed. Another Popsicle later, Elaine was fast asleep in her own bed.

CHAPTER 18

July, 1943

As spring ripened into summer, Elaine began to feel better than she had in a long while. Her throat was fully healed, and the infection, which had been draining her energy, was gone.

Fresno's fruit harvest was in full swing. Once again, freshly picked peaches and apricots were steaming out of Fresno on the Pacific Fruit Express. That special train was still being highballed down the tracks, despite the War. The military men in the East needed California's fresh fruit. Father had come home Friday evening with two boxes of apricots that he had bought cheap because they were too ripe to ship. He had managed to get them home by tying them onto the rack over the rear wheel of his bicycle.

The next morning, in the shade of the walnut tree, the Wests had an assembly line going. Billy sat with a box of apricots at his side and a bucket of water between his knees. He would take a plump, orange apricot from the box, wash it in the bucket and hand it to Sara, who was seated next to him. Each apricot had to be handled carefully, as all the apricots were so ripe they were almost soft. Each one had the blush of red that only tree-ripened apricots have. The extra days the fruit had spent on the tree gave it a tree-ripened, sharp sweetness that most store-bought fruit never had. The fruit that was being shipped to the east had been picked days before it was ripe, then loaded into boxes while it was still hard, so that it would survive the long trip and ripen just before reaching the stores. Elaine almost felt sorry for the people back east, who probably didn't even know what *real* apricots tasted like. The servicemen who ate with the Wests that summer all raved about Fresno's fresh fruit. They said it tasted so much better than the California fruit they got at home.

The whole family was hard at work under the walnut tree. Sara took each apricot Billy washed and carefully cut it in two, stem to blossom. Then, she handed it to Elaine. Elaine separated the two halves, shook the pit into a pail, and handed the halves to Mother. Mother took each apricot half and placed it carefully next to its neighboring apricot half on the top tray in the stack of old, unpainted wooden trays that sat in front of her chair. Each tray was about two feet wide by three feet long with an inch-high rim on all four sides. The trays were made just for drying fruit. Once a tray was filled with apricot halves, Father carried it up a ladder to place it on the flat roof of the garage. Here, safe and out of the way, the apricot halves would dry in the blazing sun of the always dry, rainless summer. Elaine had read in books about summer rains, but she could not imagine one.

"How come we can't just can the apricots like we used to?" she asked Mother.

"We don't have the sugar, dear." Mother answered.

"Why don't we buy some?" asked Billy.

"We need ration stamps to buy sugar," Mother explained, "and they only give us enough to buy sugar for the sugar bowl we put on the table for coffee and cereal."

The shortage of sugar probably caused the most problems for the Wests. Most of the sugar used before the war had come from Hawaii or the Caribbean Islands. Enemy submarines now hunted in those waters. Ships were badly needed to transport goods for the war effort. They could not be put in danger for something as unimportant as the transportation of sugar cane. As a result, the supply of sugar dropped sharply in the weeks after the War began. For food, the size of the ration reflected the shortness of supply, and for sugar the ration was very, very small. Mother still did some canning for fruits that did not dry well, such as peaches and plums, and crushed apples for applesauce. Mother used corn syrup instead of sugar when she canned fruit, but it didn't taste right. Before the War, Mother had made many jars of jam and jelly each summer. There had been a lot of it stored in the basement when the War started, but now, a year and a half into the War, the Wests had just about eaten it all. Mother had tried to make more last summer using corn syrup instead of sugar. But it wouldn't thicken right, and came out all runny. What little jelly and jam there was left was saved for Thanksgiving and Christmas. Now, the family just buttered their toast and the children ate peanut butter sandwiches without jelly. Some of the kids at school even started making their peanut butter sandwiches with pickle relish. But Sara, Elaine, and Billy couldn't stand that.

Just as the family was finishing their third tray, Billy scooped up a few squashed apricots. "Can we use these?" he asked, and when Sara told him, "no," he ran eagerly off toward the rabbit yard.

"Where are you going, Billy?" Elaine called after him. Billy paused for a moment, and turned. "I'm gonna give these to Thumper, 'cause I bet he'd like 'em!" Even after almost a year, and two litters of bunnies, Billy still called Thumper "he."

From halfway up the ladder, Father called to Billy. "I don't think that's a good idea, Billy. What you'll give Thumper is a stomachache!" Billy thought about that for a moment, and was just turning back to the walnut tree when he called, "Look! It's Grandpa!"

Sure enough, Grandpa West burst through the gate carrying a plain, galvanized bucket. "Look what I've got!" he exclaimed.

Billy rushed forward to go through Grandpa's pockets, searching for the candy that was always there.

"No, I mean in the bucket," he corrected.

"Why, it looks like sugar! Lots of it! Only the granules look larger." Sara said excitedly.

"It is sugar," Grandpa said, amused. "Lots of it."

"Where ever did you get it, Pa?" inquired Mother.

"Now that's quite a story," said Grandpa. "What with sugar cane being hard to get, the sugar refineries have switched to making sugar from beets."

"Ugh, beets!" Beets had never been one of Elaine's favorite vegetables.

"Not the red beets you eat, Elaine," Grandpa corrected. "No, they're a special kind of beet grown just for their high sugar content. Anyway, after the beets are made into sugar, the sugar is carried from the refinery to the packaging plant by the railroad. Somebody up the line has been punching holes in the sugar cars with a spike. So, all the way down from that point, a line of sugar spills on the ground beside the tracks as the train goes by. The first time I saw a boxcar leaking sugar I chased the train and filled my lunch bucket with sugar. Now I've taken to bringing a bucket to work with me each day. When a car goes by spilling sugar I chase it with my bucket 'till I'm out of breath."

Sara interrupted, "Grandpa, isn't that stealing?"

"Not really. We railroad men have always picked up spillage from beside the track, it's sort of salvaging. But it would sure be a crime to just let all that sugar go to waste. And the way I figure it, the thief is the man with the spike who punched the hole. I would never let my men do that! In fact, I reported to the railroad police that someone up the line was stealing sugar, but they didn't seem very interested.

"Anyways, this week I've filled two buckets. Sometimes the train goes by when we're not on duty, or stops at a siding, and there'll be a pile of sugar just lying there on the ground. I don't know how clean it is, but I used a different bucket for that and it certainly ought to be all right for baking and canning. I'm sure I can get you all the sugar you want, at any rate. There is plenty more where this came from."

"Oh, it will be wonderful to have sugar again!" exclaimed Mother. "Girls, when they finish this batch let's make the rest of the apricots into jam. And I think I'll make an apricot pie for supper."

In her mind, Elaine could already taste the peanut butter and apricot jam sandwiches that Mother would once again pack in her lunch pail when school started. And the pie they had for dessert that night was the best thing Elaine had tasted in months.

Once again, the Wests went to the redwoods near Santa Cruz for a summer vacation. But this year they left at dawn, traveling in the early morning to avoid the heat.

Elaine was delighted to find that the spring still flowed. In fact, everything was pretty much like the year before. There was only one big difference. This year they picked apples from an abandoned orchard and made applesauce. They were unable to get cinnamon so they substituted red-hot candies. Doing that not only added to the taste, but also gave the sauce a lovely pink color. So strange that the stores were out of cinnamon and sugar was rationed but cinnamon candies could be bought in every candy store. Canning seemed like much less work in the cool of the redwoods. Since they had plenty of sugar, Mother decided to can pears too. It was too hot to grow them in Fresno, but there were many pear orchards near Santa Cruz.

When it was time to go home, Father had a serious packing problem, but somehow he managed to squeeze the jars of fruit in with the people and the baggage.

CHAPTER 19

August, 1943

It was a lazy Saturday afternoon. The kids hardly noticed as they were in the shade of the umbrella tree. Elaine wasn't sure how she felt about the umbrella tree. It stood in the side yard, outside her bedroom window. At night, in the moonlight, it took on strange, even terrifying shapes so that Elaine always had to remind herself that it was only a tree. But on a hot summer day its shade was wonderful. It was always much cooler in the shade than under the brutal sun. Rae Dean, Tommy, Billy, and Elaine were making macaroni necklaces. Mother, knowing that the children were tired of all their usual summer activities, had dyed some macaroni with food coloring. They had six colors of macaroni beads to choose from. Every now and again a bead broke and had to be eaten. Elaine found it hard to decide which she preferred, stringing dry macaroni or eating it.

Whenever she felt too warm, she would go to the garden hose Father had left watering the daisies and wet herself down. The other kids did the same. Of course, they were all barefoot as usual. Elaine was wearing what she always did in the summertime: a seersucker sun suit. This one was pink with little blue birds on it. It had a pinafore top. The shoulder straps crossed in the back so they would stay up on her shoulders. Its skirt came halfway to her knees. It had a pair of full, very short matching pants that were held in place by elastic bands at the top and around each leg. Her grandmother had made the sun suit, as she had most of the clothes the children wore. Getting it wet didn't hurt it at all. As the water from her hair, skin, and clothing evaporated, which it did very quickly in that dry climate, her whole body cooled. Fresno was so dry in summertime that it was possible to feel cold even when the temperature was over one hundred degrees. All you had to do was get wet.

"I'm going to join the Marines as soon as I'm old enough," said Tommy.

"They're the ones who are winning this war, taking all those islands and such."

"It's the Air Corps bombing before they go in that's helping them." Elaine was loyal to the airmen who shared her family's Sunday dinners.

"Those planes wouldn't fly without the Sea Bees. They build the takeoff and landing strips. My dad's doing as much to win this war as any old Marine." Of the five of them, only Rae Dean had a father who was actually serving in the military.

"Yea, but the Marines are doing the killing and dying," insisted Tommy. He was right, and even Billy knew it. The Marines had been taking islands one at a time. Thousands died taking each island. The Japanese were fierce fighters, and a Japanese soldier would rather die than surrender.

Elaine left them to the argument and went to check on Lucky in her hutch. Lucky was ready to have another litter of bunnies any day now, and Elaine could hardly wait. Her last litter was almost ready to be butchered and not nearly as cute as baby bunnies were.

When Elaine saw Lucky, she became alarmed. Lucky did not look like herself. She was lying on her side, her legs all stretched out. Usually she tucked her legs neatly under herself. Her sides were heaving. Her mouth was open, her tongue lolling to one side. Elaine spoke soothingly to her, but she paid no attention. In her mind Elaine could hear the rabbit rancher saying, "With all that fur they'll die if they get too hot." There was no air moving. The other rabbits looked uncomfortable, too. Snowball's sides were heaving. Thumper had her mouth open as if gasping for breath. Elaine was afraid for them.

She ran to the house. "Daddy! Come see! There's something wrong with the rabbits!"

He came at once. They hurried to the rabbit yard.

Elaine was talking a mile a minute. "They look so hot, Daddy. The rabbit rancher said they'd die if they got too hot. They look too hot already. Don't let them die, Daddy. Can't we do something?" Her words tumbled out, one after another.

"Be quiet, Elaine, and let me think!" To Elaine, he seemed to be doing nothing. He just stood there looking—at the rabbits, at the hutches, at the yard. It was hard for her to be quiet and do nothing when she felt Lucky's life was in danger.

"Elaine," Father spoke at last. "Go to the garage and get those burlap gunny sacks, the ones that we used on the watermelons on the Fourth of

July. Let's see if they can cool rabbits the way they did the watermelons at the picnic."

Elaine ran to get the sacks. When she returned with the gunnysacks, she found her father already filling the baby bath pan with water from the garden hose. Once the sacks were wet, he nailed them on the tops of the rabbit hutches and let the wet sacks hang down over the wire sides and front of each hutch. Then he put a sprinkler head on the hose and set it to lightly sprinkle the rabbit hutches.

"As the water from the wet burlap gunny sacks evaporates, it should cool the air in the rabbit hutches," he explained. "The rabbits should be alright, but keep an eye on them just in case. You were a good girl to check on them and know when they were in trouble."

He went back into the house. Elaine stood for a while in the rabbit yard, enjoying the feeling of at last doing something to please Father. 'He even trusts me to check on them,' she thought. When she went back to where the other kids were, they were still stringing macaroni.

Each time Elaine checked on the rabbits, they appeared to be more comfortable. Their desert cooling system was working.

"I've got a nickel!" Frannie called to them as she ran into the yard. "Want to come get ice cream with me?"

"Sure!" Everybody but Tommy was eager to go.

"I don't like ice cream. It's too sweet. I want to go home anyway." And with that, Tommy went on home.

Billy and Elaine hurried into the house to get a nickel apiece and one for Rae Dean. Sara, who had felt too old to string macaroni beads, decided she was not too old for ice cream. Ice cream was always a treat and a nickel would buy a single scoop cone.

Ice cream was very difficult to store, so people generally bought ice cream immediately before they ate it. Before the war, an ice cream wagon came by every day but Sunday. Kids could hear its bell just in time to gather up some money and run to the curb before it arrived. But now, men and materials could not be spared for anything as unimportant as an ice cream wagon. Instead, the kids made almost daily trips to the creamery.

Their nickels firmly in hand, still wet from the garden hose, and barefoot, the five children set out for the Big Scoop Creamery on the corner.

"Oooh! The sidewalk's hot!" wailed Billy.

107

"Walk on the grass. It's cooler," advised Sara.

"My dad says you can fry an egg on the sidewalk when it's this hot," said Frannie.

"Ugh. I wouldn't want to eat an egg fried off the sidewalk," said Billy.

"It's just a figure of speech, Billy," corrected Sara. "We'll cross the street up there where the shade of the trees reaches almost all the way across." Before the war, the street had been busy with traffic. But now, hours would go by without a single car. The children crossed the street whenever and wherever they chose.

The soles of the children's feet were tough as leather from going barefoot all summer. Now that shoes were rationed, kids wore them only when it was absolutely necessary.

The minute they stepped out of the shade and Billy put one foot onto the black street he wailed again, "Carry me!"

The street was so hot that the asphalt paving was soft. Sara scooped Billy up and dashed for the other side of the street. "There. You're okay now," she said as she set him down on the cool grass.

By the time the children reached the creamery, their clothes were dry. It was warm in the Creamery, but the large ceiling fan kept the air moving. The only air-conditioned buildings in Fresno were the movie theaters. Billy was shirtless, and none of them were wearing shoes, but nobody cared or even noticed. People were eating sundaes and drinking sodas. They were seated at the counter in the center or at booths located along the two walls that fronted on the streets. The third side was taken up with a huge chest freezer filled with two gallon cartons of the ice cream that was made from scratch in the back of the Creamery. There were about a dozen flavors to choose from, and every once in a while the children would try out a new one. There was never a choice of cones. All cones were sugar cones, which came to a point at the bottom. On a hot day, a person had to eat fast, or the ice cream melted into the point, and then started to drip through. When that happened, the best thing to do was to switch ends, lift your chin and start eating the cone from the bottom.

Minutes later, the children were walking slowly home with their ice cream cones. On their way home they passed by the victory garden, which was bursting with vegetables. Everybody had planted too much. There was a surplus of everything to be shared with whomever wanted it. The children walked up and down the rows of vegetables and melon plants, cooling their feet in the mud of the recently irrigated garden.

"I hope we don't have eggplant for dinner again," said Billy.

"So do I," chorused Sara and Elaine. Eggplant seemed to grow particularly well in Fresno's climate.

"Our mother often makes eggplant casseroles on meatless days," Sara explained to Frannie.

"So does mine," she responded, "but today's Saturday. Monday, Wednesday, and Friday are the meatless days."

"We had fish yesterday," Elaine said. "We usually have fish on Fridays 'cause that's when it's in the butcher shop."

Mr. Schultz , the Wests' German neighbor, was in the garden. When he saw the children coming, he stopped, mopped his brow and called in his English tinged with a slight German accent, "Hot enough? Let us see now—it's Sara, Elaine, Frannie, Rae Dean, and uhh…uhh."

"It's Billy, silly," laughed Billy, amused at his joke.

"Ah yes, of course! How could I have forgotten? Silly Billy." It was a game Billy and Mr. Schultz had played many times before.

"What do you hear from Fred, Mr. Schultz?"

Fred was Mr. Schultz's son. He had left his high school teaching job and gone off to the Army Officers Candidate School last summer.. He was the only one the kids knew who would be fighting Germans instead of Japanese.

"Not a lot, except he's well and keeping busy. You know how the censors are. They never let any good information get through. But he speaks good German, you know. I'm sure the Army will use him well."

"When you write, tell him we miss him. He was always good to us," said Elaine, speaking for all the children.

"By the way, Sara, if I came down with a bucket," Mr. Schultz continued, "you think your dad would mind if I helped myself to some rabbit droppings? They make my tomatoes grow good."

"I'm sure he wouldn't mind. In fact he'd be glad to be rid of it. He's home now so just come on down and he'll help you fill your bucket."

Mr. Schultz had reminded Elaine of the rabbits, and almost at once she began to worry. "Let's get home. I want to check on Lucky."

The children said goodbye to Mr. Schultz and headed for home and the rabbit yard. Lucky was fine, as were the other rabbits, but as yet there was still no sign of little bunnies.

CHAPTER 20

September 1943

At the end of the summer, Lucky finally had her litter of seven darling little bunnies. At first they were blind, and too small to handle. Soon, however, they were old enough to eat rabbit pellets. Elaine weaned them by moving them into their own hutch, away from Lucky. Every now and then, she would take one or two of them out of the hutch, shepherding over them as they grazed on the clover in the grass. They grew so fast she thought she could almost see them grow. By the middle of September, just shortly after school started, they were almost big enough to eat. Elaine always dreaded butchering day. But when it came, it left her rich from the sale of the meat. What they didn't sell they feasted on. Elaine quickly decided that she loved the taste of fried rabbit. It was sort of like chicken, but richer and tangier. Robert, a young airman from Iowa who was the Wests' latest Sunday dinner guest, relished it also. He called it a "taste of home".

Elaine was excited to be in fourth grade. No longer was she a little kid in a primary classroom on the ground floor. Now she was upstairs with the older students. She liked her teacher, Mrs. Atkins. Mrs. Atkins was about Mother's age. Her husband, Col. Atkins, was the son of a friend of Grandma West. It seemed odd having a teacher who was married. Elaine thought teachers had to be single. Elaine had heard that Mrs. Atkins even had children of her own. With so many men going to war, there weren't enough men to take all the jobs here at home, which meant many married women had now gone to work. Before the War, neither Elaine nor Sara had known any married woman who had children and also worked outside the home. Mrs. Atkins was very strict, as Elaine thought any good teacher should be. She also assigned interesting work. That fall the students built models of Spanish California Missions and learned all about early California.

The best thing about school that year, however, was Amy Swift. Amy was a new girl in school and she and Elaine quickly became best friends. The Swifts had moved to Fresno from Yosemite National Park. In the park, Amy and her two older brothers had attended a two-room school. Elaine could hardly imagine it— grades one to four in one room and grades five to eight in another! The Swifts had moved to Fresno when a combination of gasoline rationing and the national labor shortage had caused the Park Service to cut back on personnel. The park had few visitors now. People had neither the gasoline nor the time they needed to drive there. Besides, Amy's brother was now old enough to go to high school. Yosemite didn't have a high school, so Amy's father, who was an accountant for the Park Service, moved to town. Amy lived just four blocks from Elaine, close enough to walk to, but far enough to do it only when the girls could be together for a long enough time to make the walk worthwhile. That fall, they spent almost every afternoon together, and took turns going to each other's houses after school.

One beautiful October afternoon, clear and warm, as it frequently is in the fall, Elaine went to Amy's house after school.

"Let's play paper dolls." Amy always wanted to play paper dolls. "I have a new set. They're nurse dolls. One Navy, and one Army. They have hospital gowns, dress uniforms, and civvies. They're real neat!"

Elaine didn't really like playing paper dolls, but the two of them were at Amy's house, which meant that Amy got to decide. "Okay," Elaine said, "but then let's play jacks."

They went into the house. They each got a glass of milk and a handful of the cookies Amy's mother was just scraping off the cookie sheet. They took the snacks and the paper dolls out onto the large front porch and began to play hospital. Elaine was soon bored. There wasn't much you could do with paper dolls except change their clothes. She had never been interested in clothes—not doll clothes, not paper doll clothes, not even her own clothes. Nor was she interested in nurses. She intended to be the doctor when she grew up, not the nurse. She still wanted to be a missionary doctor, like the lady in her church who was still lost in China. But Elaine would not be single, as that lady was. No, she intended to marry another doctor. Together they would have six children. She thought a large family would be fun.

Grandmother West had said she'd have to choose between being a doctor and having a family. She said a married woman couldn't have a career, or even a life of her own. She strongly recommended the single life over a life of "married drudgery." Even Mother, who was in favor of marriage, seemed to believe a woman would have to choose between a career and marriage. She said a woman could have a very full life just being a wife and mother. But just in case things didn't work out, both she and Father insisted that both girls have a college education to fall back on. For Elaine, all of that was far away, and who could tell what might happen between now and then? For all she knew, the war might go on forever, and she might need to get a job, just like Mrs. Atkins. Elaine thought about that, as she returned to her paper doll.

Amy enjoyed changing the doll's clothes. She liked clothes. She had no desire for a career. Like most girls, she planned to marry right out of high school and let her husband take care of her. Elaine enjoyed Amy's good-natured chatter, even though Elaine wasn't really listening. Elaine always felt good just being around Amy, even if it meant playing with paper dolls.

"Now let's play jacks," Elaine said after a suitable passage of time.

"Okay, if you want to." Amy never stuck too long on any one thing.

They moved to the sidewalk in front of Amy's house. The nights had been cold enough to begin to bring the leaves off of the large sycamore trees that grew in the parking strips. The girls cleared a space in the fallen leaves, swept the concrete clean with their hands, and began to play. They had each lost several of their jacks, but between them they had just enough for a complete set. When Elaine played alone, as she frequently did, she had to substitute small rocks for the two jacks she had lost since the war had started almost two years before. Another of her jacks had a broken foot but it was still better than a rock.

They used Elaine's ball instead of Amy's because the rubber of Elaine's ball had more bounce left than did Amy's. As they played, they chatted merrily.

"Are you going to the special movie next Saturday morning?" asked Amy. "It's a Cartoon special. It's free! All you need to get in is two wooden coat hangers."

"Why coat hangers?"

"Mother says the cleaners need them. Seems coat hangers aren't being made anymore either." Amy had obviously asked her mother the same question.

All at once the door to Amy's house flew open and an excited collie puppy came bounding toward them.

"Taffy! Who let you out?" exclaimed Amy as the excited puppy licked her face and swept the jacks away with her tail.

"Here, girl! Here, girl!" It was Amy's older brother, Ritchie. "I'm sorry," he said as he corralled the dog, "I didn't mean to let her out."

"It's okay," They scrambled to gather up the jacks. Some of the jacks were in plain sight. Others they found only by sifting through the fallen leaves. In a relatively short time, they found all the jacks and Amy's ball. With Ritchie's help, they continued to hunt for Elaine's ball. They hunted and hunted among the fallen leaves.

"It's got to be here somewhere," said Amy, as she sifted her hand through the leaves one more time.

They looked and looked for the ball, farther and farther away from where they had been playing. Elaine was becoming more and more anxious, beginning to lose hope of ever finding it.

"I hate to say this," said Ritchie, "but it's possible the ball rolled down the storm drain and we'll never find it."

Their faces fell. Amy and Elaine both knew he was probably right. It began to get dark, but still they hunted just in case.

As the daylight faded, Amy's mother called Amy and Ritchie into the house for dinner. Elaine had no choice but to give up the search and head for home. As she trudged home she couldn't keep from crying. She knew for sure that she wouldn't be able to get another jacks ball—not until the war was over, maybe not even then. She tried to stop crying, because she knew that if she came home crying, it would only upset everyone. But every time she thought about playing jacks in her favorite spot, that place on the hardwood floor beside the living room hearth, she couldn't help but start crying again. Aside from reading or playing solitaire, there really wasn't much else to do during an evening or a rainy day. She thought about crocheting, knitting, or embroidery, all those things Sara seemed to like, but Elaine was not good at any of those things and she didn't like doing anything she couldn't do well. Elaine was too old to play with dolls, and she'd never much liked to besides. Playing jacks was one of the few things she really enjoyed doing by herself. Now, except when she played with a friend who had a ball, her jacks playing days were over. Maybe forever.

She thought about it and caught herself just as the tears started again. She thought: 'Maybe I can learn to like playing with paper dolls.'

When she got home, Elaine stood on the porch for several minutes, drying her tears and trying her best not to look upset. When she finally thought she was ready, she went inside.

"Elaine, is that you?" Mother called as she entered the house.

"Uh-huh," Elaine tried to hold back her tears.

"You're late. I was beginning to worry," she scolded. "Why, what's the matter?" Her tone softened as she saw Elaine's tear-stained face.

"I lost my jacks ball," Elaine choked out and then ran from the room, embarrassed that she was so upset over such a childish tragedy. She tried to tell herself how minor this all was, and that friends and classmates were losing brothers, fathers, and friends overseas. What was one little jacks ball compared to all that?

Still, it hurt. Every time she thought of it, she felt like crying.

By dinnertime, she had composed herself enough not to be noticed. To help keep Elaine from crying, Mother said no more on the subject.

CHAPTER 21

October, 1943

Halloween art was hanging on the classroom walls when all the students in the school started to make Christmas cards for the servicemen overseas. They were starting early, because everyone knew how long it would take for the cards to get to wherever they were going. The children also decorated butcher paper with Christmas trees, candy canes, and stars to make Christmas wrapping paper. Around that time, the radio started broadcasting announcements that, on the first Saturday morning in November, all the kids in the city would be going around to houses in their neighborhoods and collecting combs, socks, shampoo, shaving cream, and other personal items as gifts for the men overseas. That first week in November, students took the gifts to school and wrapped them in the decorated wrapping paper they had made. Army men who were too old or sick to go overseas came around to all the schools in mid-November, loading the gifts onto trucks. By then it was six weeks until Christmas, and even though it usually took three months for mail to get through, the Army would see to it that the soldiers got the gifts on time. Everyone, including Army commanders, knew that it was important that the boys know that people at home were thinking of them, especially at Christmas.

Once the Christmas projects were finished, the students decorated the classroom for Thanksgiving.

There was a lot to be thankful for that November of 1943. Allied troops were advancing on all fronts, and although the enemy was far from defeated, the war outlook was generally hopeful.

As usual the Thanksgiving dinner was at the Wests' house. A tom turkey was roasting in the oven. Family and servicemen guests were gathering for the annual feast.

This year, Ethel—Mother's younger sister—came in the uniform of the Women's Army Corps. She looked spiffy in the gray-green uniform;

her short brown hair curled out from beneath her uniform's flat-topped hobby hat, and the gilded buttons down the front of her jacket shown like real gold. Ethel brought real cocoa and some chocolates. Such rare items were reserved for members of the military.

She had enlisted when the Army had begun accepting women into the Women's Army Corps. Women who knew nutrition and how to cook were badly needed by the Army. Many new recruits had suffered from malnutrition in their growing years, because their families had been so poor during the Great Depression. The Army hoped that good food would help get these men into fighting shape. After a brief training assignment, the Army gave Ethel the rank of lieutenant and gave her her first mission: to improve the food in the mess hall at Fresno's Hammer Field. Her first mission was a brilliant success. She enjoyed being in the WACs, and aside from complaints that the food wasn't as good as their mothers' back home, the men seemed satisfied with their meals.

Elaine was just heading out the door with her cousin to show Gladys the newest litter of baby rabbits when her Aunt Pearl and Pearl's new husband, Earl, arrived.

"Hi, Pun'kin," Earl called when he saw Elaine. "I've got something for you." He reached into his pocket and withdrew a small, white object. "Here, catch," he said as he tossed it in her direction.

Into her cupped hands dropped a golf ball.

"Your mother said you needed a jacks ball. This is the best I could do."

"Oh, thank you!" Elaine gasped as she examined her prize. "Wherever did you get it?"

"Out on base. I just beat the bushes over the fence from the officers' golf driving range until I found a ball that nobody had bothered to come after."

Elaine flew to the bare wood floor at the corner of the living room and bounced her new ball. Its bounce was perfect.

When the rest of the family and food had arrived and everyone was seated at the oddly shaped table, Grandpa West led the family and military guests in a Thanksgiving prayer. To his prayer, Elaine added her own silent prayer of thanksgiving for the used golf ball.

CHAPTER 22

February, 1944

Sara and Elaine were just finishing the breakfast dishes. They always did them together, taking turns washing and drying. Today, Elaine was the washer. The washer always finished first, and yet both girls preferred to be the drier. It was not as messy. Bright sunlight beamed in through the kitchen window. It promised to be a beautiful mid-winter day.

"I'm going grocery shopping," Mother announced as she walked into the kitchen, her handbag in her hand. "Would either of you like to come with me?"

"I would!" Elaine loved doing just about anything with Mother, but shopping was particularly enjoyable.

"I'll stay here," said Sara. "It's my turn to help daddy clean the rabbit cages. We're going to start as soon as I finish the dishes." Sara and Father got along much better than he and Elaine did. Sara and Father seemed to be able to work together as a team, whereas whenever Elaine worked with him, she seemed to irritate him, even if she tried extra hard not to talk too much. With Mother, Elaine could relax and just be herself. Mother did not care if she talked too much.

"Elaine, go get Billy's red wagon," Mother directed. "Be sure to ask him first. He is willing to share, but he likes to be asked."

Elaine found Billy in the back yard, in the bare spot under the swings. He was hard at work there, building roads for his cars and trucks. "Billy, we need your red wagon to take shopping. Can we use it?"

"Sure. I'll go get it." Off he ran, intent on his mission.

Back in the house, Mother gathered up the ration books and put them into her purse.

"Bring the fat from beside the stove and come on. I'll get the cans."

Elaine went into the kitchen and got the coffee can full of hardened fat. Each time Mother cooked meat, especially bacon, she carefully skimmed off the fat left in the pan, emptying it into an empty coffee can. The war industry used fat to make the explosive nitroglycerin, and paid ordinary citizens for their fat by giving them extra ration coupons for meat. The family also saved tin cans. When Sara and Elaine washed the dishes, they also washed any empty cans and can lids. They had to be careful with the lids, as their edges were sharp. When the cans were dry, whoever was drying the dishes cut off the bottom of the can. Then they put both the bottom and the top of the can into the can and stepped on it to flatten it into a can and lid sandwich. The family stored the flattened cans in an old gunnysack in the corner of the kitchen. Father had turned in all other bits of scrap metal when the war first started long ago.

About the time Elaine finished gathering the tin cans and the can of fat, Billy arrived with the wagon. Elaine, Billy, and Mother loaded in the cans and the fat.

Elaine took the piece of rope that was looped through the handle and tied it around her waist so her hands would be free. Then she and Mother headed off down the sidewalk to the store.

"Can, err, may I see my ration book?" Elaine asked.

Mother took one of the books out of her purse, checked the name, and handed it to Elaine. Elaine opened the little book and looked at the rows of brightly colored stamps. Each stamp had a letter on it that told when it expired. "What letter are they on now?"

"We're on 'C', dear."

"Then how come we still have so many 'A' and 'B' stamps left?"

"We don't buy many canned foods, you know that. We grow a lot of vegetables and fruits ourselves, or our neighbors do. And the ones your Father buys fresh at the farmer's market don't need ration stamps. As for the meat coupons, you know as well as I do that there is seldom any meat in the butcher shop to buy. That's why we eat so many of Grandpa's chickens and one of the reasons we started raising rabbits."

"How come there's no meat in the butcher shop?"

"Oh, probably because there are so many military bases around here. Servicemen eat a lot of meat, and besides so many cowboys and sheepherders have gone to war that there may not be as much livestock as there used to be. Also, a lot of food has to be shipped to the men in the Pacific. So, there's not much meat left for us. Still, we'll go to the butcher shop first and see what's there. I want to get rid of these cans and the fat so we'll have room for the groceries."

They parked the wagon outside the door of the butcher shop. Mother lifted the cans out of the wagon, carried them into shop, and emptied them into a large bin that stood at the front of the store. Elaine carried in the fat.

"Good morning, Mrs. West," the butcher, Mr. Sanders, greeted Mother with a smile. "What can I do for you?"

Mr. Sanders was a large, slightly overweight man with graying hair. He was standing behind the meat cases, which were almost empty. There was a little lunchmeat, a few cheeses, and very little else.

"I'd like two pounds of cheddar and a pound of bologna please, Mr. Sanders. Oh, and slice the bologna and half of the cheese for sandwiches, if you could."

Mr. Sanders tore a piece of butcher paper off the roll in front of him and put it on the scales beside the meat case. He took out a block of cheese and sliced it the way Mother wanted. As he wrapped the cheese he said, "I hope everything is going well with you and your family."

"Yes it is, thank you," Mother replied.

As he stooped to get another piece of butcher paper he noticed Elaine. "How are you, Elaine. Still liking school?"

"Yes, it gets more and more fun all the time."

He shook his head. He had once told Elaine that he had never liked school and couldn't understand how she did. He sliced, weighed, and wrapped the bologna. He noted the cost on the package. "Anything else? I have some nice liver."

"I'll take a pound of that," Mother said. "It will do for tonight's supper."

It was no surprise to Elaine that he had liver left. She hated it, and guessed that a lot of airmen did too. She made a mental note to play at Amy's house that afternoon and see if Amy could get her mother to ask her to stay for dinner.

"Do you have any bacon?" asked Mother. "Or beef?"

"No beef," replied Mr. Sanders. "But I have some bacon in the back that I save for my regular customers. I'll sell you a pound."

"I'll take it."

Mr. Sanders walked to the back room to get the bacon. When he brought it in it was already wrapped and priced.

"Also, I brought in some fat." Mother took the can of fat from Elaine and placed it on the counter. Mr. Sanders weighed it, subtracted the weight of the can and figured the ration points. "I can give you eight points off the bacon for the fat," he said. "By the way, when is your husband going to bring me more rabbit fryers to sell? People keep asking for them."

"We have a litter that will be ready for butchering in a week or so. We should have five extras. He'll bring them over. I'm glad people enjoy them".

'People might enjoy eating them,' Elaine thought, 'but Father sure hates butchering them.' He would always put it off until finally Mother had to threaten him. "John, if you don't kill those rabbits this weekend, I'll butcher them myself." Somehow, the very idea of making Mother kill anything was worse to Father than doing the job himself. He would take the knife and go out into the rabbit yard at the next opportunity.

Once, and only once, Elaine had quietly followed Father so she could watch. First Father grabbed a rabbit by its hind legs, held it upside down, and gave it a sharp strike on the back of the neck with his hand. Then, quickly, he cut off the head and cut the skin around each leg, slit the back end around the tail and peeled the hide off the rabbit as if he were taking off a pullover sweater. He then put the skinned rabbit into a pan.

By the time Father brought the pan full of dead rabbits into the kitchen, Elaine had an easier time thinking of them as food. By then, Elaine was even willing to help Mother prepare them. Mother carefully washed each one, cleaned out the insides, and washed it again. Then she put the liver and heart back inside the rabbit. Elaine wrapped each fryer in wax paper and set it aside. The first two of the fryers went into the refrigerator to be cooked later, and Father sold the rest to the butcher. The owner of the doe who had mothered the litter was paid for each rabbit that was butchered, whether it was sold to the butcher or eaten by the family.

Mr. Sanders had finished wrapping the liver. "Will that be all, Mrs. West?" he asked.

"Yes, for today."

Mr. Sanders totaled the cost of each item on a piece of paper, and then showed Mother the total so she could check his addition. She nodded then handed him the money and the required ration stamps. He put the ration stamps into a box under the counter, and punched the money amount into the cash register. The bell clanged as the cash register door slid open and Mr. Sanders counted out the change.

"Good day, Mrs. West," said Mr. Sanders, and closed the cash register door.

"Good day," responded Mother, and put her purchases into her shopping bag.

Elaine pulled the wagon with Mother's shopping bag down the street toward the grocery store. They walked past the cleaners and the vivid, dark red entrance to the Chinese restaurant. They stopped briefly at the drug store. While Elaine waited outside with the wagon, Mother went in for soap and toilet paper. They continued down the street, and passed the barbershop where Father got his hair cut. Elaine slowed down at Al's Tobacco and Candy Shop, lagging behind so she could carefully size up the candy in the window. Elaine frequently spent her small allowance on candy there. Although sugar was so scarce that it was rationed, candy was still plentiful, and Al's had the best selection. Oddly enough, except for the chocolate that came from imported coco beans, candy remained plentiful throughout the war.

Next, they passed the five and dime store. It was called that because much of what was sold there cost only a nickel or a dime. It was another place Elaine spent her rabbit money. She bought comic books, ornaments, junk jewelry, and other kid stuff there.

By now they were under the canvas awning that shaded the door and window of the grocery shop. The wood and glass door stood open, but the screen door was closed to protect the interior from flies. They left the wagon outside the door and went in. A large oscillating fan just inside the door helped keep the store slightly cooler than the outside. It was a large store, almost as big as Elaine's classroom at school.

"Good morning Mrs. West, Elaine," said Mr. Wright, the grocer. "What can I do for you today?"

"We're doing a lot of shopping today," said Mother.

"Let me get a boy to help you then," said Mr. Wright. "Ralph, come help this lady."

A husky stock boy who looked to be about fifteen came out of the back room. He carried an empty cardboard box. He followed Mother while she walked between the shelves and chose the items she wanted to buy: cereal, rice, flour, dried beans, pasta, canned tuna, peanut butter, and bread. She grabbed butter from the small refrigerator case. Butter used to be delivered with the milk, but now that it required ration stamps, the dairy no longer bothered with it. When the box was full, Ralph carried it to the counter and came back with an empty one. By the time Mother finished her shopping, the second box was almost full. Ralph put it on the counter in front of Mr. Wright and went back to refill the shelves.

Meanwhile, Elaine studied the contents of the small glass-topped chest that contained the only frozen foods she knew: ice cream bars and Popsicles. Elaine knew she couldn't buy either on this trip, as it would spoil her appetite for lunch. But she might want to come back later with some of her rabbit money.

Mr. Wright totaled the cost of the groceries on the adding machine. He knew every price by heart. This was not too difficult, because prices were set by the government and had not changed since the war began. Mother sometimes added the cost of each item in her head so she would know what the total should be. Like Elaine, she enjoyed doing arithmetic in her head. Once Mr. Wright had figured the total, he rang up the amount on the cash register that sat on the counter. Mother wrote a check for the amount.

Next, Mr. Wright totaled the ration points. Totaling ration points was a more difficult job than totaling money. The number of ration points needed to buy an item changed with the supply and demand for that item. When there was a doubt as to the number of points an item cost, Mr. Wright referred to the chart he had clipped from the newspaper. One by one, Mother tore the necessary ration stamps from the books and gave them to him. He put them into a box under the counter. He would have to sort them all out later and turn them in to the Office of Price Administration in order to get more rationed items to sell. "I sure don't like this rationing business," he grumbled. "It makes a lot of extra work for me. By the way," his tone brightened, "Is your husband still working at Fort Stockton?"

"Off and on. But somebody from his office goes up there at least once or twice a week. The Army has to keep enlarging the Prisoner of War camp there. They keep getting more and more German prisoners from North Africa." Mother had a pretty good idea why Mr. Wright was asking the question.

Mr. Wright continued, sheepishly, "Ah, I wonder if he could get my radio fixed. I hear those German boys are good at fixing things. All the local repair shops have closed because of the war."

"Oh, I'm sure he can. Those prisoners are all sitting around up there, just waiting out the war. They're all so anxious for the work that they'll take just about anything. They can always use money for cigarettes or candy."

"Just a minute. I'll get it from the back room. Ralph, help Mrs. West out with her groceries." With that he disappeared into the back room.

Ralph had the groceries loaded into the red wagon by the time Mr.

Wright arrived with the large radio. "Thanks so much. We're lost without our radio. We don't know what's going on, 'cept from the paper. Besides we really miss President Roosevelt's fireside talks. He always makes us feel better about the war. My wife will be so pleased that I've found someone to fix it." With that, he crowded the radio in with the groceries. Then, he motioned Mother over and Elaine noticed that he held a couple of small cans in his hand. "Here," he said, "let me see that tuna you've got." Mother handed it to him, and he handed back one of the cans he'd recovered from the stockroom. Mother was surprised. "Canned salmon! From Alaska?" Mr. Wright winked at her. "We do what we can. Consider it a free upgrade, in exchange for the radio."

Mr. Wright followed Elaine and Mother outside and adjusted the awning to the changing angle of the sun. "Have a nice walk home," he called and returned to his store.

"Are we going to the bakery?" Elaine asked.

"No, I already bought bread at the grocery store. It's not as fresh as the bakery bread, but it will do. I'll be glad when we can buy sliced bread again. I get so tired of slicing it for sandwiches and toast."

"How come they don't sell sliced bread anymore?"

"The government outlawed it as a labor-saving measure. But," Mother added, "It sure doesn't save my labor!"

"When we get home may I go over to Amy's?" Elaine asked, remembering the liver in the wagon.

"Just as soon as all these groceries are put away and after you've had some lunch. It's not polite to go to someone's house just before meal time."

"What's for lunch?" Elaine thought the liver was for the evening meal but she wanted to be sure.

"Soup and sandwiches," Mother replied.

Elaine heaved a sigh of relief. As they trudged home, pulling the wagon full of groceries, Elaine was deep in thought. She had heard that many children in the war-torn countries of the old world were hungry for anything to eat. No doubt they would have been very grateful for just some of the food in Billy's red wagon. Maybe even the liver.

CHAPTER 23

April, 1944

It was springtime in Fresno, and all over town the sycamore trees were sprouting new leaves. The children had been a bit slow that morning and got to school as the bell started ringing. They had to run to line up.

Once all the students were in the classroom and the second bell rang, they stood to salute the flag and then sing. It was the Marines' hymn this time:

"From the halls of Montezuma
To the shores of Tripoli"

Elaine loved geography, but she had no idea where the halls of Montezuma or the shores of Tripoli were. Once the morning ritual was over, they settled down to their lessons.

Their elementary school was getting crowded. Two classes had moved into the old auditorium, so now even small assemblies had to be held in the lunchroom. There were no empty desks in any of the classrooms. New kids had to be seated at the reading table. And new kids kept coming, as more and more people moved to California. No new houses were being built, so newcomers crowded into old ones. There was a terrible housing shortage. Wages were high, so newcomers could afford a place to live; the problem was in finding one. Many people were discovering that they really could "do better" in California, just like Grandpa West said.

Now that Elaine was in the fourth grade, the desks in the room were screwed to the hardwood floor in long lines. The seats, too, were fastened to the desks. The first desk in the line had no seat fastened to it. The seat for that desk was fastened to the front of the desk that was second in line, and so on. At the end of the line was a seat with no desk. Since her last name began with a "W", Elaine had the next to the last seat in the last row. She sat just in front of Jimmy Wong. She expected to go through the rest of her school career seated behind Danny Taylor and in front of Jimmy Wong.

Elaine had always liked Jimmy. His family had been in California as long as hers had. This was much longer than the families of most of the kids in the class. The Chinese community in Fresno was very large—one of the largest in the US. In fact, it was second in size only to the Chinese community in San Francisco. Although many of the Chinese lived in one section of town, called Chinatown, other Chinese families were scattered throughout the city. The Chinese were an accepted and respected part of the community, as American or Californian as anybody. And the Wongs, who owned a restaurant in Elaine's neighborhood, were all well liked.

On the other hand Danny, who sat in front of Elaine, was a real pain. He never sat still and when he wiggled it shook her desk because it was attached to his seat. If she complained, he banged his knees together deliberately to rock her desk even harder. Still, sometimes Danny would play tic tac toe with her. He was always the one who got in trouble when they did this, because he was the one not facing forward, and because he was a boy.

Elaine quickly finished with her reading lesson and began reading a comic book Danny had slipped to her. Comics were not allowed at school, so she hid it in her spelling book. If Mrs. Atkins happened to glance her way, she would think that Elaine was studying her spelling. Mrs. Atkins would be pleased at that, because she knew Elaine was a poor speller. Elaine was not overly fond of comic books, but enjoyed getting away with a forbidden activity at school. The day had gotten off to a good start. She hoped it would continue, and that Mrs. Atkins wouldn't cry today.

Mrs. Atkins cried a lot. Some days, she would sit at her desk and cry and cry, for hours on end. The first time Mrs. Atkins started to cry, Elaine and the other students all wondered what they'd done wrong. After a while, the children understood that it had nothing to do with them. In fact, as long as no one did anything too noisy, Mrs. Atkins seemed to forget the class was there. Students could do pretty much as they pleased. But, after a while they all began to wish for school as usual. They were tired of reading comic books, playing hangman, and drawing on the blackboard.

Even the students who didn't like subjects like reading and arithmetic got tired of only getting fun subjects, like art, music, and especially P.E., on the rare days that Mrs. Atkins felt up to teaching them. What shocked Elaine even more was that the principal, Mr. Carpenter, knew all about it. He would stick his head in every now and then, and so long as there were no fights, he didn't do a thing.

When Elaine first told Mother about the situation, Mother seemed alarmed. "What do you mean, she cries?"

"She just cries. First, she just looks very sad. She just stares off into space. After a while, tears start to stream down her cheeks. Then she starts to sob softly; finally she just puts her head down on her folded arms and cries herself to sleep.

"Does she do this often?"

"Not too often," Elaine lied. She liked Mrs. Atkins, and did not want to get her in trouble.

"What do you kids do?" Mother had been a teacher, and knew that students took advantage when no one stopped them.

"We just take care of ourselves. Sometimes there are assignments on the board and we do those." Elaine didn't tell her what else they did, but she bet Mother pretty well knew. Mother had a saying: "When the cat's away, the mice will play."

Mother looked sad and shook her head. "I hope you don't take advantage, Elaine. The poor woman has more trouble than she can handle."

"What do you mean?"

"Well, she and her husband have a turkey ranch just outside of town. Her husband, Captain Atkins, was in the National Guard. He was sent to help defend the Philippines and hasn't been heard from since."

"Was he in the Bataan Death March?"

The Bataan Death March was one of the most troubling stories to come out of the Pacific in months. Although it had taken place when the Japanese first took the Philippines in the spring of 1942—when Elaine was in second grade—news of it had not reached America until last January.

Mother answered Elaine's question with one of her own. "How do you know about Bataan?" Mother seemed a bit upset by Elaine's question. She, like other grownups, tried to keep the most unpleasant war news from the kids. But everyone in town knew someone who had been on Bataan. Lots of people were talking about it, and Elaine had listened.

Elaine continued, "I know the men captured on Bataan were forced

129

to walk to a prisoner of war camp, and that a lot of them died on the way. So what happened to Mrs. Atkins' husband?"

"That's what nobody knows, Elaine. Mrs. Atkins doesn't know if her husband is alive somewhere, if he was killed in the battles, or died on the march or after he got to a prison camp. She just knows that she hasn't heard anything about him since Bataan."

Elaine thought Mother's account was finished with that. But after a while, Mother sighed, shook her head from side to side and continued. "I think it may be harder to live with not knowing than to live with knowing the worst."

After that, Mother asked almost every day how Mrs. Atkins was. Elaine had to admit she was crying more and more often. By that May it was almost every day.

Recess at school was still fun, even though there were no longer any balls to play with. The last ball in the school had blown its patch the previous month. Elaine took her jacks bag from her desk and lined up for recess. In school, one always traveled in a line, although when Mrs. Atkins cried her class didn't bother.

Today, Elaine was out on the playground with Amy and a small group of other girls.

"Let's jump rope, Elaine," Amy suggested.

"I'd rather play jacks." Elaine was not very good at jumping rope.

"We can do that after school, when there's just the two of us," reasoned Amy. "Jump rope's more fun with lots of people."

"People" meant girls. Boys might jump rope in their own neighborhoods, but not at school. At school, they played marbles on the dirt schoolyard, or some rough chase game such as war. War was an updated version of "king of the hill." It was played in teams, defenders against invaders.

"C'mon, Elaine. We can play jacks later!" Amy persisted.

"Okay," Elaine agreed. Jumping rope with the other girls was better than playing jacks alone. Since the jumping order had already been established as first come, first served, Amy was at the end of the line. Elaine had to turn one end of the rope while a girl who came after them turned the other end. Each girl's turn lasted as long as the rhyme she chose to jump to. If she missed by stepping on the rope or stopping the rope with her body, she lost her turn and had to take an end of the rope. Soon, someone missed, and Elaine gave her the rope end to turn and took a place in the jumping line behind Amy. After a while, Amy was jumping, while everyone chanted:

Charlie Chaplin went to France
To teach the ladies how to dance.
First on the heel, then on the toe,
Round and around, and around you go.

Amy whirled round and round while she jumped. She made it look so easy.

Salute to the captain, bow to the queen.
Do the splits, and never more be seen.

Now it was Elaine's turn. She called for *Teddy Bear*. She managed to jump in without a miss.

Teddy Bear, Teddy Bear, turn around.

She turned around as she jumped.

Teddy Bear, Teddy Bear, touch the ground.

She touched the ground and so it went.

Teddy Bear, Teddy Bear, tie your shoe.
Teddy Bear, Teddy Bear say, "Adieu."

She tripped on the rope on the way out. But, before she could take an end and turn, the bell rang. Recess was over.

Mrs. Atkins cried all afternoon. It was really boring. When Mrs. Atkins fell asleep, Elaine joined the girls who were playing jacks on the floor in the back of the room. They talked about what they would do at Girl Scouts after school. Like most of the girls, Elaine had worn her Girl Scout uniform that day. She loved Girl Scouts. They did such interesting things. Everyone liked the scout leader, Mrs. Conley. She was younger than their mothers. She had the cutest baby girl, named Annabelle. Sometimes Mrs. Conley brought Annabelle to their meetings. When she did, the girls took turns watching her. Watching a real toddler was a lot more fun than playing with dolls.

After school, the girls hurried to the lunchroom where Girl Scouts would meet. On the way, Mary Jo dropped her sweater. Elaine scooped it up and threw it to Amy. They laughed as Mary Jo ran after it. But Amy threw it to another girl and on the game of keep-away was on. By the time they got to the lunchroom, everyone was running, yelling, and laughing.

"Girls, girls!" Mrs. Conley called. "Sit down so we can get started."

Nobody paid any attention. They were having too much fun.

"Girls! Girls!" She tried again but no one seemed to hear her. They just kept running, laughing, chasing.

"Okay," she said, "if you don't want a Scout meeting, there is no sense in my staying." And before they realized that she was leaving, she was gone.

All at once things didn't seem so funny. Everyone felt terrible. They had actually chased her away. "Maybe," Rae Dean suggested, "if we all sit down and be quiet she might come back." They did just that, but it didn't work. She didn't come back.

"What if she never comes back?" thought Elaine. "How could we have upset Mrs. Conley so much? Will we ever have scouts again?"

No one was laughing now. The custodian came in and told them to leave.

"Where can we go?" asked Rae Dean. "If I go home now, my mother will ask why I'm home so early. What can I say?"

"I'll be in trouble, too," said Amy. Several of the other girls said the same.

"We can all go to my house," offered Mary Jo. "My mother plays bridge and won't be home 'til after scouts are usually over."

They all started out for Mary Jo's. The overcast sky matched their mood as the girls walked sheepishly on their way.

"I smell tar," said Rae Dean, her voice brightening.

"Let's get some," said Mary Jo.

The girls followed their noses until they found the tar. There it was, a barrel of tar, simmering over a small gas burner on the side walk. On the roof of a nearby house a man was spreading melted tar onto the roofing. Most of the girls broke twigs off a nearby bush. Each stuck the twig into the melted tar and pulled out a glob of tar, waited for it to cool a bit, but not too much, and then stuck it into her mouth.

'Ugh," shivered Carol Ann. "I don't see how you can stand to chew that stuff!"

"It has more flavor than wax," said Elaine.

"Remember when there was real chewing gum?" Rae Dean chimed in, before popping the tar into her mouth..

"Yea, those were the days," Amy said.

"What happened to all the gum?" Mary Jo asked.

Elaine had an answer for her. "Mother says that, like rubber, it's made from South American tree sap."

"Oh. That explains it," Mary Jo said. "C'mon, let's go before someone sees us."

The girls chewed tar as they went on to Mary Jo's house.

When the time Scouts was usually over came, the girls all started walking home. When she got home, Elaine walked into the house as if she were coming home from scouts.

"Elaine," Mother called from the kitchen. "Come in here. I need to speak with you."

'She knows,' Elaine thought.

"Where have you been? Mrs. Conley called. What do you have to say for yourself?"

"I'm sorry. I was at Mary Jo's. We all just sort of got carried away. I'm really, really sorry." Elaine knew no excuse would help and besides she couldn't think of one.

"I'm sure you are. But that doesn't help much. What are you going to do about it?"

"I'll apologize to Mrs. Conley and hope she accepts it. I'll do it now." Elaine headed toward the phone.

"No, you'll do it in writing." Mother knew that Elaine hated to write letters. Elaine could never think of what to say or how to say it in words she could spell. "And you'll do the dishes alone for two weeks, one week for upsetting Mrs. Conley and one week for not coming straight home. Now, start writing. And use the dictionary as you go. Every word must be spelled properly."

As Elaine headed to get the dictionary from the bookcase in the living room, Sara's grinned and made a face at her. Elaine pretended not to see her. She didn't really blame Sara. After all, Sara had just gotten out of doing the dishes for two whole weeks.

By Memorial Day of 1944, the US and her allies were closing in on Germany from Italy in the south and from Russia in the east. An invasion from the west, from Britain into France, was expected soon.

The battles in the Pacific were a different matter. With every push, with each tiny island that the Americans wrested from the Japanese, casualties numbered in the tens of thousands. At Elaine's church, the number of silver stars on the banner shrank, even as the number of gold stars grew. Everybody knew the tremendous cost of winning the war in the Pacific, but nobody talked about it.

That Memorial Day, the family took the bus downtown to Courthouse Park. They sat on the grass around the courthouse and listened to the military band. Everybody stood as the honor guard from Hammer Field paraded in with the flag, while the band played "Stars and Stripes Forever." Everyone pledged to the flag and sang "The Star Spangled Banner." They stayed standing while a large lady with a larger voice sang "God Bless America." Then they sat down again to listen to the speeches. The mayor spoke of the thousands of brave men who so far had given their lives for their country. Elaine thought of Andy and the growing number of gold stars on the banner on her church wall. A minister prayed for the many thousands of men waiting in England, ready to invade France and chase the Germans out. Elaine thought of her friends and classmates' relatives: fathers, uncles, brothers. She thought of their neighbor Fred Schultz. He had already been gone so long that Elaine wasn't sure she'd recognize him when he came back, if he came back. A trumpeter bugled *Taps*. The commemoration was over.

D-Day—the invasion of France from Britain—came on June 6th, 1944. In the days and weeks that followed, no one had any idea exactly how many men had died. All people knew was that Americans were fighting the Germans in France, Belgium, and Holland. Everyone was waiting to hear that his or her loved ones were still alive. It was a time of hope and a time of dread. School was out when people began to hear some of what had happened at D-Day. Thousands of men, both Allied and German, had lost their lives in the landing. Fierce fighting followed the invasion, and for weeks nobody knew who would win. But by late summer, the Allies had a foothold and were advancing through France. Mr. and Mrs. Schultz were terribly worried about their son Fred. They did not know if he had been part of the invasion or not, but it made sense that he would have been. After all, he spoke excellent German and could interpret when needed or sneak behind enemy lines, or even become a spy by stealing a uniform and posing as a German soldier. As days went by and they didn't hear that he had been killed, they began to assume he had survived the landing. In war, no news was good news.

Germany would be defeated, but not easily. It was not yet time to celebrate. It was time to mourn the thousands of dead.

CHAPTER 24

July, 1944

School had been out for three weeks. Elaine was still enjoying being able to do what she wanted to most of the time. She still had chores, of course. She had to feed and water the rabbits, do the dishes, and help with the laundry and cleaning. She also cooked dinner one night a week, with Mother's help of course. It was practice so that she would know how to cook when she had a family of her own. Many evenings, the whole family would go down the street and work in the victory garden. But Elaine didn't really think of that as work. Many of the neighbors were there, and people often just stood around and talked. The victory garden brought the whole neighborhood together.

And then there were special projects, like canning. Sara and Elaine had been helping Mother can peaches all morning. The peaches had come from one of Grandpa's neighbors. He had brought them over early that morning, and some of them were too ripe to can. Those, Mother and Elaine made into jam, now that they had lots of sugar. The sugar trains were running again, and being spiked, and Grandpa had brought another bucketful of sugar with the peaches. Canning was a hot job, and the kitchen was all steamed up. They had finally finished with both the jam and the canning around noon, and were cleaning up for lunch.

After lunch, Amy and Rae Dean were coming over so that they, Elaine, Sara, and Billy could all go to the movies. Elaine went to the Saturday afternoon matinee at the Tower Theater whenever she could. There were usually a lot of kids Elaine knew there, some from the neighborhood and some from school. It was so beautiful inside! Neon birds, butterflies, trees and flowers glowed softly on the walls. Elaine loved the Tower Theater. For only twenty cents—a penny more than the cost of a loaf of bread— she could spend an entire Saturday afternoon in its enchanted darkness. The Tower Theater was especially nice in summer because it was air-conditioned. Just cooling off was worth the price of admission. Elaine even liked the newsreels. They helped her understand the news she heard on the radio every morning and evening, which was almost always about the war and often talked about places she wasn't familiar with.

Billy often took a long time to eat his lunch, but that afternoon, Elaine didn't really mind. It didn't matter much what time the kids left home, because they could miss the start of the movie if they had to. Actually, Elaine didn't even know when the movie started, and anyways it didn't matter. Movies played in a continuous loop, so people could come into a movie in the middle and just stay until the beginning came around again. Once a person was inside the theater, he or she could stay as long as he or she wanted to, or until the theater closed. That afternoon, the theater was showing a new Roy Rogers film and *Lassie Come Home*, which the kids had all seen for the first time last year. Rae Dean and Elaine loved Roy Rogers. Billy and Amy loved dog stories. Sara loved Gabby Hayes and the Sons of the Pioneers. And on the newsreels, there would probably be something about what our armies were doing in France. The cartoon might be Bugs Bunny or Donald Duck. Everyone would have a great time.

"Girls, Billy," Mother said as they came to the lunch table, "I'm afraid you won't be able to go to the movies after all."

"But why?" Billy asked. They were all disappointed.

"The health department has closed all of the theaters. I just heard it on the radio."

"Why would they do that?" asked Sara.

"The polio epidemic has gotten worse. More children are getting sick every day."

"What's that got to do with the movies?" Elaine asked.

"Polio is very contagious. It spreads from person to person. The best protection against it is to stay away from other people, especially children, because they are the ones that are most likely to be carrying the germ. So the health department has closed those places where children go in large groups. Theaters, playgrounds, swimming pools... they're all closed until further notice as of this morning. I just found out about it myself. Anyways, you will be safer if you just stay here and play."

It all seemed so unfair to Elaine. Kids start getting sick, so the grownups take away every fun thing they can do. On the other hand, though, Elaine could not remember when she had not been afraid of getting polio. Mother had told her the real name of the disease once: "Poliomyelitis". But Elaine couldn't even begin to pronounce that, and besides everyone just called it infantile paralysis. It was called that because most of its victims were children and often the victims were left paralyzed. The disease attacked the body's muscles and often crippled them, and since the heart was a muscle and muscles ran the lungs, it could kill its victims. President Roosevelt himself had suffered from the disease, although he always looked healthy in the newsreels. He had started the March of Dimes to raise money to fight the disease. The money from that was also used to build special hospitals and to buy wheelchairs and crutches for the surviving victims. They also used the money to buy iron lungs. Elaine had seen a boy in an iron lung only once, in a newsreel. It was a huge machine. It covered most of the boy's body as he lay in it, so that only his face and arms showed. Elaine wondered how a person could live like that, trapped inside a huge machine. The March of Dimes advertisements made everyone aware of the horrors of polio. Posters of children on crutches, in wheelchairs, or imprisoned in iron lungs were almost as common as war posters. The pictures fed Elaine's fear.

A few days later, at the victory garden, they heard that Warren, Frannie's thirteen-year old brother, had infantile paralysis. Frannie's family had gone to Santa Cruz on vacation. On the way over, Warren had kept saying that he wasn't feeling well. His parents thought it was just a combination of the heat and carsickness. He kept saying that his legs hurt. His parents thought it was just because his legs were cramped by the ice chest on the floor of the back seat of the car. But when they arrived at the beach and he went to get out of the car, he fell and could not get up. The family panicked, and rushed him to the nearest hospital. He was still there, in the hospital in Santa Cruz, and they said he might never walk again. His mother and Frannie had stayed in Santa Cruz to be near him but after a week their father had returned home to go to work. He had brought the news.

The news frightened all the children, especially Elaine. "What's going to happen to Warren in the hospital? Will he be all right?" She found it hard to wait until her first question was answered before asking another.

"I'm not sure." Mother answered.

If Mother wasn't sure he would be all right he might not be. Her fear grew.

"What's going to happen to Warren?"

"He'll probably be all right." Mother was trying to reassure her but still be truthful. "He'll get the Sister Kenny treatment. It often prevents paralysis. He'll probably be all right."

"The Sister Kenny Treatment?" In her mind, Elaine saw an image from one of the posters, of an elderly nun bending over a boy in one of the wards. In the poster, the boy looked terrified and helpless.

"It was invented by an Australian nurse. Nurses are often given the title 'sister'."

"What is it? What do they do?"

"First, the nurses put very hot, wet compresses on the affected muscles. Then they massage and exercise them."

"How can that cure a disease?"

"It doesn't. The disease just runs its course. Rest and good food are the only medicines we have. Sometimes a person is left paralyzed, sometimes not. Sometimes the Sister Kenny Treatment prevents the paralysis."

"How do you get it, again?" Elaine was more worried and frightened than she wanted to let Mother know.

"Doctors think you breathe in the germ, but no one knows for sure. They have not been able to find the germ, so the doctors suspect it is a virus. Not much is known about viruses, because they're too small for us to see, even with a microscope. Warren will probably be all right. Everyone's doing all they can. All you can do is pray."

Elaine knew from Mother's tone of voice that the conversation was over. She went to play with the other kids at the victory garden, but her thoughts kept returning to Warren. She had never liked him much. He was always teasing the younger kids and doing mean things, like hitting their croquet balls down the street so that they had to run after them. One time, when they were playing hide and seek, he had just gone home and left everybody hunting for him. But even though Elaine didn't want to play with him again, she didn't want him to be paralyzed.

That night Elaine had the first nightmare she'd had in a long time. She awoke screaming, "I can't walk! I can't walk!"

"Elaine! Elaine! Wake up! You're having a bad dream!" Sara shook her fully awake, but Elaine was still terrified. "My legs hurt. They hurt awful! I can't walk! I know I can't walk!"

Now Sara was frightened. She ran to wake up Mother.

Mother came. She felt Elaine's brow. "You don't seem to be feverish." How's your stomach?"

"It's alright. It's just my legs," Elaine whimpered.

"How about your head and neck? Do they ache?"

"No. It's my legs. I can't walk."

140

"There, there, Elaine. You're all right," she comforted. "You don't have a fever. You're not ill. If you had polio you'd feel bad all over. It's just a bad dream. I know you can walk. Just try. Just put your feet out. That's right. Over the side of the bed. That's a good girl. Feet down on the floor. Now put your weight on 'em. Lean on me. Now stand. Now walk. See? You're all right. You can walk. It was just a terrible dream."

Now, fully awake and half way across the room from her bed, Elaine felt foolish. She thought herself too old for nightmares.

"I'm sorry. I didn't mean to cause such a fuss. Sara, Mother, I'm sorry I woke you up."

"It's all right, Elaine. Just go back to sleep."

She did, after a while. But the dream came again and again.

Not long after Elaine had the first dream, she called Rae Dean to see if she could play. Rae Dean's mother, Mrs. Medley, answered the phone. When Elaine asked for Rae Dean, Mrs. Medley began to cry. Between her sobs she told Elaine the news. Rae Dean was in the hospital. She had infantile paralysis, too.

It was hard to believe. From all the crying Mrs. Medley had done on the phone Elaine knew Rae Dean was very, very sick.

Although Elaine now considered Amy her best friend, Rae Dean was her oldest friend. Elaine had known Rae Dean since before she could remember, and they still played together a lot. Try as she might, Elaine just couldn't imagine Rae Dean in one of those hospitals. People could die from polio, after all. The next day Elaine saw Rae Dean's picture in the newspaper. "Local Girl at Death's Door," the story caption read. Rae Dean had the most serious form of the disease, polio bulbar. She was still breathing on her own, the article said, but they had put her into an iron lung, just in case. The article said there was no cure, not even a good treatment for the disease, and so it had to run its course. Only time would tell whether she would live or die. Elaine feared she might never see her friend again. There might not be any more fun times together.

Elaine thought about their last quarrel. Rae Dean had wanted to play at her own house, but Elaine had left to go play at Amy's house instead, and Rae Dean hadn't been allowed to go, because she was being punished for what had happened at Scouts. Rae Dean and Elaine had always quarreled a lot, and after the last one, Rae Dean had said for the thousandth time, "I'll never speak to you again." Elaine remembered thinking then, 'oh, but you will,' because that's how Rae Dean was. But now, Rae Dean might not ever speak to Elaine again. The article went on to say that, if Rae Dean recovered, she might not be able to breathe without the help of a machine. How could they play jacks if Rae Dean was in an iron lung?

Through it all, Elaine couldn't help but feel awful about the way she'd treated Rae Dean.

Every day, Mother called Mrs. Medley to get the latest news. Every night, Elaine had the nightmare. Then, little by little, the news got better. It was a miracle, but Rae Dean seemed to be fighting her way back to health. Each day Mrs. Medley sounded more hopeful.

One day, about two weeks after Rae Dean had gotten sick, Elaine decided to make a card for Rae Dean. She settled down at the dining room table with paper, crayons, and scissors. Just as she was finishing up, Mother came in. "I spoke with Mrs. Medley again this morning. She said that Rae Dean's doing much better, and when I told her about the card you were making, she said she'd deliver it for you. You can run it over to her anytime today."

After lunch, Elaine walked over to Rae Dean's house and knocked on the door. Mrs. Medley answered cheerily. "Elaine! Come on in!" Elaine entered, and she was amazed at what she saw. Scattered around the living room were cards, toys, and baskets of candy, all addressed to Rae Dean. "Some of these," Mrs. Medley pointed to the packages, "are from friends or relatives of Rae Dean. But most are from people we don't even know." Mrs. Medley showed Elaine all the toys that Rae Dean was still too sick to play with: new dolls, balls, and board games. She even had a brand new jacks set, with a brand new red rubber ball. Elaine hadn't seen any of these things new since the War started. Rae Dean even had a new girl's bicycle, with new tires. Mrs. Medley said the toys, even the bicycle, had come from people who had read about Rae Dean in the paper. It made Elaine feel a little better, that even total strangers cared that much about Rae Dean.

As it turned out, within weeks Rae Dean was out of the iron lung. The doctors said that she was no longer contagious, and was well enough to have visitors. She was transferred to another part of the hospital, a special section for children who were recovering from polio. Sara and Elaine were invited to visit, but Mother said that Billy was too young. Mrs. Medley had received a special gas sticker that allowed her to buy the gasoline she needed to visit her daughter, and she drove the girls to the hospital with her on her next visit.

On the way out, Elaine thought about what Rae Dean might look like after five weeks of being sick. She remembered seeing a girl at school who had gone bald from Scarlet Fever. She thought about the posters again, the ones with kids on crutches and in wheelchairs. Elaine decided she'd be happy to see Rae Dean, no matter what she looked like. Still, she prepared herself for the worst.

The hospital was a large, solid, four-story brick building. It looked very much like a large school. The girls followed Mrs. Medley in through the double doors and up to the counter. Mrs. Medley gave her name and said the girls were also visitors. They were directed to a nearby door that led outside, to the back of the hospital. Outside, they saw a sign with the words "Poliomyelitis Ward", and an arrow on it. They followed the arrows until they came to a gate. Rae Dean was waiting with a nurse on the other side of the gate. The recovery ward wasn't anything like Elaine had imagined. In fact, it was almost like school, complete with a playground. There were several children already playing there.

Rae Dean looked just the same as when Elaine had last seen her. She hadn't lost any of her hair, just a little weight. Elaine ran to her and hugged her. "Oh, Rae Dean! I'm so glad to see you! You look great."

Elaine was so relieved. Rae Dean had not lost her hair. She wasn't on crutches or in a wheelchair. She seemed to breathe just fine. She had not changed a bit.

The grassy playground had swings, slides, and even a small merry-go-round. Nearby, several children were playing noisily. Elaine thought it looked like a really fun place. She wondered what Rae Dean thought of it.

"What's it like here?"

"It's awful! Oh, the food is real good. The nurses and everyone are really kind. But the hot towels are too hot. Kids scream and cry all the time, and we can hear it all. I can hardly wait to get home! But I got some wonderful presents. I got a whole carton of chewing gum from the man at Jerry's Tobacco and Candy Shop. He saved it up, just for sick kids like me. I passed gum out to all the kids in the ward, but I have some left." She pulled a package of gum out of her pocket and held it out to us, "Here, you can each have a piece. And take one home for Billy."

Elaine could hardly believe her eyes. She had not even seen a real piece of chewing gum in years.

"Gee, thanks!"

"Yeah, thanks," agreed Sara

Elaine unwrapped the gum and shoved it into her mouth. It tasted wonderful! If she was careful, and left it in a safe place when it was not in her mouth, she could chew it for days.

"Do you know these other kids?" asked Sara.

"Most of them. Some are just visitors, but most are patients like me. It's not too bad, really. We're all going home soon anyway."

The girls played happily for about half an hour. Then it was time for Rae Dean to go back inside.

After her visit to Rae Dean, Elaine's nightmares stopped. Her visit had made her more hopeful, and less fearful.

That August, Father was given a week's vacation. Instead of going to the coast, the family decided to go camping in the mountains. Father figured that would be easier on the car's tires, which were now completely bald. The family could leave in the morning and be out of the valley and into the mountain shade before the road got really hot. Elaine loved camping. She could escape not only the heat, but the war as well. It seemed as if the only change the war had brought to the mountains was better fishing in the lakes and mountain streams, probably because there were fewer fishermen. It was easy, too, for Elaine to forget there was a war on until they went to visit the power plant. Elaine had really looked forward to once again seeing the water roaring through the giant turbines. She could barely remember her last visit, from before the war. She was disappointed, however. The power plant was under armed guard, and closed to all visitors.

When Father's vacation was over, they returned to the valley. Rae Dean was still in the hospital but Warren was back. He seemed to be just fine, except that he had to take long naps. Elaine quickly noticed that his illness had not improved him a bit. He was still as mean to the younger kids as ever. A week after that, Rae Dean finally came home. By then, the pools, parks and theaters were all open again. The epidemic had passed, and news of the War was the only news.

It was like nothing had changed.

CHAPTER 25

September, 1944

Labor Day came and went without much celebration. No one had enough gasoline to escape the heat by going to the mountains or the seashore, and there was lots of labor to be done. The grapes were ripe! The radio was begging for pickers. "Grape pickers are urgently needed to bring in this year's crop. There will be free transportation from Courthouse Park to the vineyard. Ranchers are offering eighteen cents a tray-- a two-cent raise over last year. Wear trousers, a long sleeved shirt and a hat. Bring your own knife, drinking water, and lunch. Bus leaves at 6:00 A.M., returns at 3:00 P.M." Sara and Elaine, being city kids, thought grape picking sounded like an adventure. Mother had grown up on a farm, and knew better. She tried to tell them it was hard, hot work. She told them if they did it they would have to promise to finish the vineyard or at least work a week. The girls kept insisting that they wanted to work. They promised they would not quit, but would work hard for at least a week. Mother finally agreed. She was still not sure it was a good idea, but she thought the experience would be good for the girls, and it would help the ranchers.

Saturday, Elaine went with Mother to the five and dime store where they bought three grape knives. The knives looked just like the short, thick-handled knife a man used to cut linoleum. That evening Mother helped the girls select and lay out the proper clothing. She made sandwiches for lunches, and filled the water jug.

It was just beginning to get light when mother woke them the next morning. They tumbled out of bed, dressed for grape picking, breakfasted, and headed out to the bus stop. Mother carried the water jug, and Sara and Elaine carried the lunch Mother had packed. Billy carried a bag of his cars and trucks to play with while they worked. Elaine dozed on the bus; when she awoke they were at Courthouse Park. She was not used to getting up so early. There was a crowd of people at the park, lining up for the school buses parked on the street. Mother and the girls got into one of the buses. When it was filled with people, it left. Sara and Elaine, excited about having a job, chattered merrily on the short ride to the fields.

"Look! There's an Army bus!" Billy exclaimed as the bus they were riding in slowed and parked. Ahead of them was a parked farm truck from which two men were unloading wooden drying trays. Other men were carrying the trays down the rows of vines and laying them down on the dirt in a long line. The men all wore black shirts with the letters "POW" stenciled on them in big, white letters.

"Are they Army men?" Billy pointed at the men.

"Yes," Mother answered, "but not our army. They're German prisoners of war. The radio said that they were doing the heavy work of the harvest this year."

"But couldn't they just run away?"

"Where would they go?" Sara said. "Besides, they have guards. There they are." She pointed to the two men in Army fatigues, sitting in the shade of some vines.

Elaine watched the Germans. They looked like anybody else, not scary at all. One man seemed to be in charge of the others. "Is that one the boss German?" She pointed at the man who wasn't doing any of the work himself.

"Probably," Mother said. "I heard they work under their own officers."

"But why would they help us?" Elaine asked.

"Why not? By now, they must know that Germany is going to lose this war. They can always use the money they get, or save it until the war is over. Besides, after almost two years of being in the camp, they are probably glad to get out of it, even if it is to work in the sun."

While Elaine was watching the prisoners, a man came up and demonstrated how to harvest the grapes. He held a bunch of grapes in one hand and cut the stem from the vine with one stroke of the curved bladed grape knife he held in the other hand. He laid the picked bunch on the wooden tray that lay on the dirt between the vines. He demonstrated again with another bunch of the small yellowish-green grapes to show them how close together the bunches must be placed on the tray. He told them they were to reach through the vines to get every bunch of grapes off each vine. Elaine was not paying close attention. She was too interested in the prisoners. The rancher then began assigning rows to families. The row assigned to them seemed to stretch on forever.

Mother gave Sara and Elaine each a knife. They were to work on the vines on one side of the row while she worked on the other. At first, it was fun. Elaine and Sara raced to see who could pick grapes faster. After a while, though, it became work. The vines were dirty and made Elaine's hands itch. There were wasps everywhere. She was afraid of being stung. Her stomach began to hurt from all the grapes she had eaten. Her back hurt from reaching for grapes and then bending to put them unto the tray. The work got harder and harder.

The rancher—or maybe his foreman, Elaine couldn't tell which—came by and told her that she hadn't filled the trays properly. The grapes had to be closer together. She had to empty one tray in order to properly fill the others. Elaine decided she would save time if she did it right the first time. Sara was much faster than Elaine, and Mother was faster still. As the morning grew old ,it began to get really hot. The heat made the work even more difficult.

Finally, Mother decided it was time to break for lunch. By this time there was almost no shade, as the sun was too high in the sky. Elaine didn't feel at all like eating, but mother said she should eat anyway.

"How do the grapes turn into raisins?" Elaine wanted to delay going back to work as long as possible.

"The grapes dry in the sun." Mother suspected her question was a delaying tactic, but being an ex-schoolteacher she couldn't resist a chance to educate. "When they are half-dry men flip them over onto an empty tray so they can dry on the other side. That is really hard work, as the wooden trays are heavy, especially when they are filled with grapes. This year, German prisoners will probably be used to flip the trays. After more time in the sun the grapes are thoroughly dry. Men stack the trays, one on top of the other. They cover the stacks of trays with a tarp to let the raisins sweat until all the raisins have equal moisture content. After that, the raisins go to the packing plant."

They rested a bit more and then they went back to work. In a short while the combination of eating too many grapes, the hot sun and the hard work made Elaine really sick. She threw up her lunch.

Mother gave her permission to rest in the shade the rest of the day. She walked to the end of the row, back to the road where the bus was parked and crawled in under the vines, leaned her head against a stump and watched the prisoners working a short distance away. They seemed cheerful, sometimes singing, sometimes calling to each other in German, sometimes even laughing. She thought of the stories her father had told them about the prisoners when he had worked at Fort Stockton. In exchange for their promise not to run away, the prisoners were housed in "honor camps" with almost no guards. They lived in the camps under the leadership and direction of their own officers. Father had called them "Rommel's Boys." Field Marshal Erwin Rommel had been mentioned in the news on the radio almost every day early in the war. He was Hitler's most famous general. Elaine's favorite story was one told to Father by one of the soldiers guarding the camp. "It seems they had taken a bunch of Rommel's boys into town to get some library books. When the bus left to take them back to the camp, one of the prisoners was in the rest room. When he came out he saw everyone was gone. He was really upset. He didn't want to break his promise not to run away. Besides, he had nowhere to go. So he started hitchhiking back to the camp. Even though he had a huge white 'POW' stenciled on the back of his black shirt, he got a ride and made it back to camp in time for roll call."

At the time, his story had been very comforting to Elaine. The Germans had captured one of her school friend's brothers. It was natural for her to assume that American prisoners in Germany were being treated just as well. Now, she was not so sure. She wondered if the Germans were mistreating prisoners, as, according to the radio, the Japanese seemed to be. 'Probably not,' she hoped. These Germans seemed so much like the American airmen who shared their Sunday dinner. Did they, too, have families back home that they missed? One of the prisoners working across the road kept looking at her. He walked to the edge of the road and smiled and waved to her. Elaine waved back. All at once he sprinted across the road toward her. He said something to her but his English was poor and she didn't understand him. His officer yelled at him. The officer sounded angry. The prisoner tossed something to her, saluted the officer, and ran across the road toward him. Mother was suddenly there, questioning her.

"What did he throw to you?" She sounded out of breath. She must have been running.

Elaine held out the package of lemon drops the young man had tossed to her. Mother relaxed and shook her head from side to side as if to say so much fuss over so little. The German officer left the prisoner he had been yelling at and walked over. He clicked his heels and bowed to Mother.

"Pardon, Madam," he said. "Excuse the boy. He is not meant to frighten you. He is, how you say, homesick. He has a smaller sister in the Faterland. Again, excuse please."

"I understand," said Mother. "Elaine, would you like to thank him for the lemon drops?"

Elaine nodded. "Yes!"

Mother turned to the office then. "Will you call him over?"

"Hans! Kommst du hier!"

The young man ran back across the road, clicked his heels, saluted the officer, and bowed to Mother.

"Thank you for the candy," Elaine said, smiling at him.

The German officer translated.

The young prisoner, Hans, bowed to Elaine. "Bitte shein, Mädchen." His face held a huge grin.

"How old is your sister?" asked Elaine.

The officer translated.

"Zehn Jahre." Hans lowered his head a bit, and added, "ob sie noch leben."

"He says she is ten years"

"He added something else." Mother had caught the under tone. "What was it?"

"If she lives. He is from Hamburg. From your radio we know it is bombed hard and often."

They were all quiet for a while, and then Mother asked the officer, "Do you have a family?"

"Yes!" he smiled and pulled out a photograph. He showed it to Mother, then to Elaine, then Sara and Billy, who had joined them by this time. In the photo, a smiling woman stood next to two young boys and a younger girl.

"Nice looking family," Mother said. "How are they getting along?"

"I do not know. We get no word from home. They are near Berlin. I hope the Americans get there before the Russians. You Americans are generous, and kind. The Russians, they are not so. Good day, Madam. Thank you for talking with me. Pardon again, for the boy." He bowed again and then the Germans walked back to their side of the road.

Mother and Sara went back to work. Billy stayed with Elaine. The German soldiers were indeed a lot like the airmen who were the Wests' Sunday dinner guests, a long way from home and missing their families. But there was a big difference. The fear that the US might be bombed was all but a thing of the past; our airmen were going into danger themselves, but they knew their families were safe. These Germans, on the other hand, were safely out of the war, but they worried because their families lived in constant fear of injury and even death. Elaine thought about this difference as she watched the prisoners work in the sun; finally, she nodded off to sleep. She was awakened when a man came to count their filled trays. The picking day was over.

Elaine really didn't want to pick grapes ever again, but Mother insisted. She said, "When I was your age, there was a year when we sent our crop to market and it didn't sell. All we got for a year's work was a bill for the freight charges. Raisin ranching is a risky business. If the grapes aren't picked in time to dry before the rain comes, then the rancher has no income. He needs our help, little as it is. Besides, you promised to pick for a week. It won't be so bad tomorrow. Pace yourself and don't eat so many grapes. You should be all right."

They worked the rest of the week. Elaine watched Mother and copied her movements. She didn't mess around but stayed right on the job. Like a machine, she would grab a bunch of grapes, cut it from the vine, lay it onto the tray in a smooth but swift motion, then repeat the action with the next bunch. The number of trays Elaine filled each day went up. She didn't get sick again. But, by the end of the week she didn't ever want to see a grape again, let alone eat one.

CHAPTER 26

November, 1944

It was autumn in Fresno, and the sycamore trees were shedding their leaves once more. The neighborhood kids kicked the fallen leaves out of their way as they walked to school. Rae Dean and Elaine were in charge of the daily walk to school, now that Sara was in junior high. While the younger children curb walked, or did other kid stuff, Rae Dean and Elaine, now in the fifth grade, walked on the sidewalk with dignity. They took their duties seriously.

Tommy no longer walked with them. He took a different route, one that had more boys on it. School was pretty much the same as last year: the same kids (with a few new ones), and the same room arrangement. But this year, they had a new teacher, Miss Bodkin. She was much older than Mrs. Atkins, who was not teaching anymore. Miss Bodkin was tall and thin with grey hair knotted into a bun on top of her head. No stray strand of hair ever dared to escape. Her blue eyes looked right through you if you tried to make excuses. She must have had eyes in the back of her head, because she knew what was going on in the classroom, even when she turned her back to write on the blackboard in front of the class. Like most teachers, Miss Bodkin had never married. It was hard to imagine her ever crying. With Miss Bodkin in charge, the students did a lot of their work in front of their classmates, on the slate blackboards that covered two of the classroom walls. Any mistake a student made was immediately visible to Miss Bodkin and everyone else. At these boards the students worked examples in arithmetic, language, and spelling. Elaine liked doing arithmetic at the board, because she was good in that subject and it gave her a chance to show off. Elaine hated working at the board in language and spelling, because she was a poor speller. She was embarrassed to have everyone see her mistakes. But then, Elaine had always been a good student overall. 'How awful working at the blackboard must be for Danny Taylor,' she thought, 'he isn't good at anything.'

The school almost never had air raid drills anymore. The war was too far away. The school had become very shabby, too, because nobody had painted anything or made any repairs to the building since the war started. Even the school building seemed tired of the war. The wooden desktops were pencil-marked and grooved. The schoolyard fences were down in several places, but that didn't matter much now anyway. The fences were there to keep the balls from rolling into the street and there were no balls left now. And these days, instead of singing military fight songs after the flag salute, students would request songs like *Coming in on a Wing and a Prayer,* or *Waltzing Matilda,* a favorite of the Australian allies. Elaine's favorite was a song they'd learned from the radio

> *When the lights go on again*
> *All over the world*
> *And the boys come home again*
> *All over the world*

Like everyone else, Elaine wanted the war to be over. President Roosevelt, whose fireside chats were heard over every radio in America, had convinced everyone that the best chance for a lasting peace lay in defeating and then occupying both Germany and Japan. A negotiated peace with Germany would not guarantee that Germany would not rest, rearm, and attack again, as it had after the last war. Nothing less than Germany's total and unconditional surrender was the only way to bring democracy to Germany and peace to Europe. Even the German prisoners knew Germany would eventually lose the war. Still, the fighting and dying went on.

It was Friday. Friday was stamp day. A lady from the office came to the classroom and sold government-issued savings stamps. By buying savings stamps, kids lent money to the government. A student could buy them in ten- or twenty-five cent denominations. The student then pasted the stamps into a special book. It took seventeen dollars worth of stamps to fill a book. When the book was full it could be traded in for a United States War Bond that would be worth twenty-five dollars in ten years. Elaine always spent some of her rabbit money on savings stamps. She had already traded in one book of stamps for a bond. As she stood in line to buy more stamps, Elaine thought back to Pearl Harbor Day, so long ago.

She remembered how back then she hadn't known the difference between a bomb and a bond. But then, so much had happened since.

The rabbit business was still good. Although the newer airplanes had heated crew areas, the fur-lined leather flight jackets were still regular issue to flight crews in the older planes. Mr. Sanders, the butcher, was still very eager to buy any rabbit fryers the Wests had to sell. Beef, pork, and lamb had more or less disappeared.

Friday was also the day Miss Bodkin filled the students' inkwells with black ink. There had been an ink hole in Elaine's desk since she was in third grade, but she had always done all her schoolwork in pencil. Finally, now that she was in fifth grade, she was given an inkwell to go into the hole. It was a little glass bottle, with a steel flip top. Every Friday, Miss Bodkin came to each desk with the tin ink pitcher. The ink pitcher was shaped like a watering can, but it was smaller, and thinner, and it had a lid. Its spout was longer and tapered at the end. Miss Bodkin walked down the aisle between the desks and carefully poured a small amount of ink into each inkwell. When all of the students had ink, a monitor passed out the hard finished ink paper, dip pens and blotters. Any writing the students did on Fridays, they did in ink. Today, instead of just practicing their penmanship, they were asked to copy a letter they had already written in pencil onto good ink paper. This would be their "pen pal" letter.

Earlier in the week, each student had drawn a letter from a basket. Each of these letters had been written by a student in Britain. Boys had drawn from boys' letters, and girls from girls' letters. Then, each student had written a letter in reply to the letter he or she had drawn. Miss Bodkin said that writing to a student in another country would make the world a friendlier, more peaceful place. Elaine had drawn a letter from a girl named Elizabeth. Elizabeth lived in Manchester. Elizabeth said she loved Western movies and wanted a pen pal from the West. She had all sorts of questions about cowboys and Indians. Elaine had written her reply on the thin, soft surfaced, light tan newsprint paper that they used for ordinary work. She had explained to Elizabeth that she lived in the city and never saw any cowboys or Indians. Elaine told her that she also loved western movies, but they were about the past. She told Elizabeth about how her Grandfather had been born in Kansas during an Indian raid. But such Indian raids never happened anymore. As for the cowboys, they were probably off fighting in the war like everyone else.

Today, Miss Bodkin had returned a corrected version of Elaine's letter for copying. Elaine used her best writing, carefully blotted the ink, and handed her letter in to be checked by Miss Bodkin. Elaine hoped Miss Bodkin would judge it good enough for mailing, so she wouldn't have to copy it all over again. Miss Bodkin wanted each letter be properly done. She said the reputation of American schools was at stake.

The Polio scare had ended, and so far had not returned. Elaine went to the movies almost every Saturday. With the rabbit money, she could well afford the ticket price. Every week, there was an updated newsreel. The summer before, the newsreels had shown pictures of D-Day—of American men charging up French beaches, into the face of German machine guns. It made Elaine proud, frightened, and sad all at the same time—proud that American men were fighting and dying to free others from tyranny; frightened and sad, because she knew that somewhere in the US, there was a broken family for each fallen soldier.

Elaine now followed the progress of the war eagerly. The newsreels showed more now than they had earlier in the war. Now, the enemy knew only too well what weapons the Allies had. Elaine saw film clips of American tanks and infantrymen slogging through mud in France. She saw French civilians cheering and throwing flowers, and even kissing American GIs as they liberated French villages and cities. One newsreel showed an American regiment made up entirely by Japanese-American men. They had just rescued a unit of Texan National Guardsmen who had been trapped behind German lines. "Japanese-American" was a new term. It was a term of respect, first used to tell the difference between the Japanese who were fighting with the Allies, and those fighting with the Japanese enemy. The pictures of those tall Texans hugging those short Japanese Americans reminded Elaine of Miko. Elaine realized how long it had been since she'd thought about Miko. What was Miko's life like now? Did she have a relative fighting in Europe while she and her family were still imprisoned behind barbed wire? Nearly three years earlier, when Miko had gone into the camp, Japanese-Americans had been despised, beaten up, and called "Japs", "Nips" and worse. Now that Japanese-American troops had fought so well and so bravely they were no longer considered enemies. That made Elaine wonder, 'Why are there still Japanese families in camps?'

CHAPTER 27

January, 1945

Throughout the war, the Wests had continued to have servicemen to their home for Sunday dinner. This Sunday's guest, Herbert, and Father were talking while the girls were helping Mother with the dinner. Elaine and Sara were setting the table. Elaine was working in slow motion so she could listen to Herbert talk. His English was interesting. Not at all what Miss Bodkin would have considered correct, but interesting just the same. And Herbert looked so young! Elaine decided she would try to find out how old he was before the day was out. Elaine noticed Herbert kept looking at Sara. Sara seemed a bit flustered. She kept looking at him to see if he was looking at her. The girls finished setting the table and returned to the kitchen about the time Mother began to put the food into serving dishes.

Once the kitchen door was shut, Elaine turned to Mother and asked, "How old do you think Herbert is?"

"Well, you have to be seventeen to enlist," Mother answered, "and he's finished basic training, but he could still be only seventeen. He does look awfully young. Here, Sara, carry in the green beans."

"You do that." Sara nudged Elaine. "I'll soak the pots and pans."

Mother gave Sara a questioning look, and then she helped Elaine carry in the food.

Dinner was awkward. It was hard to keep a conversation going.

Herbert talked about his family, about the corn they grew and the pigs they raised. He talked of his brothers and sisters. One of his sisters had just gotten married.

Elaine was still interested to know Herbert's age, and so she asked: "How much older than you is she, Herbert?"

"Oh, she's my little sister. She's fifteen."

Elaine was stunned. In her family, a girl couldn't even be alone with a boy on a date until she was sixteen. Before she could think of anything to say, Herbert turned to Sara and said, "Miss Sara, maybe you and I could go to the movies this afternoon."

All chewing stopped. Elaine looked at Herbert, then Sara, then Father, then Mother. Sara's face was beet red. She seemed to be as surprised as Elaine was.

Mother, however, was neither surprised nor upset. "Sara is much younger than she looks," Mother told the soldier kindly. "She is only thirteen, much too young to date."

No one else said anything. Father was furious. He stabbed the meat on his plate with his fork, then picked up his knife and cut his meat with short, swift strokes. His mouth was set. The family had learned long ago how to tell when Father was angry. He didn't say anything the rest of the meal. Sara kept her head down and ate slowly, taking only small bites. Elaine tried not to laugh while she watched the other people at the table. Mother's expression was pleasant, but her eyes lacked their usual warmth. Herbert didn't know what to do. He just sat there, shame-faced, trying to figure out if he had broken some unspoken rule. Elaine admired the way Mother kept the conversation going, smoothing over Father's silence. Billy, who knew something was up but didn't have a clue what it was, just sat with a puzzled look on his face.

Once the meal was over, Mother sent Sara and Elaine to the kitchen to do the dishes. She told Billy to carry the dirty plates, forks, and glasses from the table to the kitchen. To Elaine's surprise, Father, still angry, jumped up to help Billy. He then busied himself with putting away the leftovers leaving Mother in the dining room with Herbert. Normally, Father entertained the guest while Mother saw to the leftovers. About the time the girls finished the dishes, Mother came into the kitchen to tell everybody that Herbert had left to walk to the bus stop.

At that news, Father finally exploded "That's it! "No more soldiers in this house! To think he thought an invitation to a meal was an invitation to date my daughter! I'll not issue any more invitations!"

Elaine thought the whole thing was too funny for words. She teased her sister unmercifully. But whatever fun she got from teasing her sister was not worth the loss of the servicemen guests. Elaine was not alone in missing the Sunday visits. Everyone, including Father, was sorry that chapter was closed.

On February 23rd of that year, *Life* Magazine came out with a picture of half a dozen U. S. Marines raising the American flag atop a mountain on a tiny, remote Pacific island. That island was called "Iwo Jima." Iwo Jima was an island of only eight square miles—one-third the size of Manhattan— and yet twenty-one thousand Japanese soldiers had died at Iwo Jima while defending an airbase. Only two hundred Japanese had surrendered, and most of them were too wounded to fight on. The Allies had suffered great losses also, but many of the twenty thousand allied casualties had merely been wounded. Island by island, the Allies were creeping up on Japan. But the Japanese refused to surrender, even when they knew they were beaten. The cost in human life of taking the home islands of Japan would be enormous, and everyone knew it. Once again, Elaine thought back to the pictures in the D-Day newsreels—beaches littered with dead and dying men—'but,' she thought, 'once they got through to mainland France, the French people helped them.'

In Japan, there would only be enemies. Elaine realized, then, why all the grownups seemed terrified.

The Tuesday after St. Patrick's Day, when she got home from school, Elaine found Mother in the midst of putting together a package to mail overseas. In the specially marked box, Mother had packed a small canned ham, a tin of spam, some canned tuna, and some chipped beef. Those items alone took a good part of their monthly meat ration. She had added some tea (also using a lot of ration stamps), dried apricots, raisins, sugar, and canned milk. In the corners she squeezed in wrapped candy. She also included soap, combs, toothbrushes, and toothpaste.

"Who's it for?" Elaine asked.

"Elizabeth's family," said Mother. "Manchester was really hit hard by the German bombs early in the war, and some thereafter. They've gone without for so long. Now that the U-boats are no longer a worry, we can help them out a bit—keep their spirits up until the war is over."

Elaine was proud of Mother's generosity.

That April, President Roosevelt died. It was a great shock to the world. No one had even known he was ill. In newsreels, he had always looked the picture of health. He was widely loved, and even those who had not voted for him respected him. To Elaine, Roosevelt was *the* President. He had first been elected two years before she was born. Only last November, he had been reelected for a fourth term—no President before had served more than two! Like everyone else, Elaine didn't know how the country would get along without him. Most of the adults had no confidence in his successor, Harry Truman.

Why, Truman hadn't even gone to college!

CHAPTER 28

May, 1945

Spring had come to Fresno once more, and Elaine was just weeks away from the close of her fifth grade year. And so, one lazy Friday afternoon, Elaine was sitting at the dining room table, pasting comic strips onto sheets of typewriter paper. She had been carefully cutting them out of the newspaper each day. She had written the date on the margin of each strip so as not to get them out of order. Now, she was assembling them into homemade comic booklets for the soldiers and sailors in the hospitals. One booklet would be of *Popeye,* one of *Dick Tracy,* and another of *Blondie.* When they were finished, each booklet would have several weeks' worth of comic strips, in the order in which they were first published. She wanted to finish them this weekend so she could take the comic booklets to Girl Scouts. Her troop was making the booklets as a service project.

Mrs. Conley had accepted the girls' apologies and agreed to continue as their leader. Elaine enjoyed Girl Scouts even more this year, now that they were doing so many service projects. Making comic booklets was just one of these projects. They also wove blanket squares, which would be used to make lap robes for men who were now in wheelchairs. Elaine busied herself with projects now, instead of playing jacks. Jacks were for little kids anyway. Sometimes, the girls in the troop went down to the Red Cross Headquarters and helped to pack Red Cross Boxes. Doing this was like working on an assembly line. Each member put one item, such as a bar of soap or a tin of Spam, into the white box with the Red Cross emblem on it, and then passed the box to the next person in line. These boxes were not going to soldiers. They were going to the war-torn areas, to help the local people who now needed them so badly. Once the boxes were full, older volunteers loaded them onto trucks.

That Saturday, the Tower Theater showed "State Fair" and a Roy Rogers movie. Between the movies they showed the latest newsreel. In it there were pictures of a place called Dachau. It was a camp of some sort, surrounded by tall, wooden fences topped with barbed wire, with a huge factory-like building in the middle of it. There were row upon row of shabby wooden barracks. But it was the pictures of the people in the camp that shocked Elaine to her core. Elaine could only glance at the horror on the movie screen before she got too sickened and had to turn away. She had to force herself to look again, to see if she had really seen what she thought she had. It was difficult to believe such cruelty to other humans was possible.

The films showed sunken-faced living skeletons of all sizes, lining up for dishes of food being handed out by grim-faced GIs. Other human skeletons—fully grown men and women who were too weak to stand—sat or lay on the bare ground. Some of these living skeletons were being fed like babies. The newscaster, his voice choked with emotion, said that they were too weak to feed themselves. Obviously, something monstrous had taken place there, but the newsreel gave no explanation as to what or why. The newsman said this was just one of many such camps that the Allies had recently overrun. He called these places "Death Camps." He told how in many camps, people were ushered naked into showers where poison gas came out of the showerheads. He spoke of ovens, where prisoners were forced to burn the corpses of other prisoners.

The whole thing was almost beyond belief.

On May 1ˢᵗ, a strange rumor circulated in Fresno. The rumor was that Adolf Hitler—Germany's hated leader, who had brought war and misery to Europe six years before—had been killed while leading his troops. Few believed it. But just one week later, on May 8ᵗʰ, Germany surrendered. As it turned out, Hitler had shot himself in the head while hiding away, safe in a bunker. There was a huge celebration in downtown Fresno, but the Wests didn't go. Father thought that the crowds would be too rowdy for kids. And, from what Elaine heard about the celebration from the kids at school who did go, it was. Germany was out of the war, and yet nothing much changed in Fresno that summer. The lights were still off, and still, the men stayed overseas.

The war would not end until the Japanese surrendered, and so far surrendering was not something the Japanese had ever done. The Americans had pushed them off dozens of islands and, with the help of the British, Chinese, Australians, and other Allies, out of most of East Asia. And yet, the Japanese fought on. The only option left to the Allies now was to invade the home islands of Japan. Everyone was talking about it, especially Father. And everyone agreed on one thing: the invasion of Japan would be far, far bloodier than the invasion of France had been. After D-Day, the civilian population in France and Belgium had risen up against the Nazis and helped the Allies fight the Germans. In Japan, there would be no friends, only enemies. The Japanese boasted they would arm every man, woman, and child—with clubs and pitchforks if need be. And if the Japanese would die in such numbers for tiny chunks of rock in the middle of the Pacific, invading and occupying the home islands would be a nightmare. Japanese casualties were expected to number eight million. Three million of these would be soldiers, and the rest just ordinary people. The Allied casualties would probably number a million or more.

That amounted to one hundred men for every American, Canadian, and British soldier who had fallen at D-Day.

It was Tuesday—the day before Memorial Day—and all over Fresno flowers were in full bloom. The early morning was cool, but the sun shone brightly, promising a warm day. In the hour before school started Billy, Mother, and Elaine were in the yard, gathering some of those same flowers.

"Billy, you pick the daises," said Mother. "Get as long a stem on them as you can. Elaine, you pick the sweet peas. I'll get the roses."

"How come we're picking the flowers today when Memorial Day isn't until tomorrow?" asked Billy. He was in second grade now and much more talkative.

"Because it will take a day to get all the flowers gathered and taken to San Francisco," replied Mother.

"Who's going to put 'em on the graves?" asked Billy.

"The paper said the school children of San Francisco will do it," said Mother.

"How come they need so many flowers?" asked Elaine. "My teacher said they're sending them from all over California."

"They're for the casualties," explained Mother. "From all the islands we've had to take back from the Japanese. Those boys are gone now, and their families will never be the same. It's the best we can do to see to it that they are buried on American soil, and that their graves are cared for. I don't know whose idea it was to have children gather flowers for the graves, but I think it's a good one. I hope they do it every year."

Elaine thought of Andy. He would never be buried on American soil. His plane had gone down at Midway, and his body was never found. She tried to remember what his face looked like, but couldn't. Elaine tried to remember all the other airmen, too. There had been so many of them since the war began, Elaine didn't remember their names anymore. She just thought of them as airmen. Now, she wondered how many of them were buried in California. She also wondered how many of them there were who, like Airman Andy, would never be buried at all.

Mother continued, "One of the country's biggest military cemeteries is on a green hillside overlooking San Francisco Bay. For each body of a man buried on that hillside there is a white cross. Tomorrow, there will be a bouquet of flowers beside each white cross." She paused when she saw Mrs. Schultz coming, carrying a large shopping bag.

"Hello, Gertrude" Mother said warmly. "I bet you're enjoying having Fred home." The neighborhood was buzzing with the news that Fred had come home a few days ago on a medical discharge, but none of the neighbors had seen him since. No one knew why he had been given a medical discharge. It was a mystery.

Mrs. Schultz smiled. "Yes we are, although he hasn't done much but sleep since he got here." She held out the shopping bag to the children. "Here, Elaine, Billy. I want you to take these to school, too."

Elaine and Billy were amazed. Mother had told them more than once not to go anywhere near Mrs. Schultz's roses. The flowers were delicate and very special to Mrs. Schultz. Some days, she spent hours in her rose garden, tending to the plants. She never let a child in her yard unless they were accompanied by a parent, and even then she would watch them like a hawk, and ask them not to come too close to the roses. She got very upset if a cat or dog wandered in there. Now, she was simply giving away her prized roses.

"I'm so lucky my boy came home; so many didn't," Mrs. Schultz continued, "I love my flowers, but keeping them now just seems selfish. After what those boys went through, what they and their families have given up. What are my roses against all that? Now, you children be extra careful when you take these to school. When you put them in water don't touch the petals. Touching the petals makes them turn brown. And make sure to tell the other kids that, as well. You know how special these are to me, and I'm trusting you, Elaine, to take care of them. You're in charge now."

Elaine swelled with pride as the weight of responsibility settled on her shoulders. She gingerly took the bag from Mrs. Schultz. "Don't worry," Elaine said, "I'll take real good care of them. And I won't let anyone else ruin them. I promise. And say hello to Fred for me. I'm glad he's home."

When the flowers were all picked and wrapped in newspaper, they waited in the shade for Rae Dean. When Rae Dean came, she also had her arms full of flowers. Billy, Elaine, and Rae Dean started out toward the school. On their way, they spotted other groups of kids, traveling in twos or threes, arms full of flowers.

In front of the school, Army trucks lined the street. On the wide, concrete school steps were dozens of empty one-gallon tin cans, each half full of water. Billy and Elaine filled several cans with the flowers from their bags. Elaine was careful to put Mrs. Schultz's roses in a separate area of one of the cans, and leaned them away from the steps so that nobody would touch them. A soldier was helping with loading the truck, and Elaine made a point of telling him to be careful with the roses. Then, her duties over, she stood in a spot just off the steps and watched the Army men at work.

Other students came by and filled other cans. Soldiers in fatigue uniforms loaded the flower cans into the trucks and replaced the empty space on the steps with more cans, ready for more flowers. It was a happy, bustling scene. Once again, Elaine thought of Andy, and where the flowers were going, and felt both happy and sad, all at once.

Over the next few minutes, several other students joined Elaine at her spot by the steps. They all stood, silently watching, until the principal herded them into the building.

The war in Europe was over, but the American soldiers were still there. Allied troops were busy helping Europe change back to civilian rule. In the case of Germany, the Allied generals were actually governing the country. Europe was a mess. The newsreels showed roads, bridges, railroad tracks, canals, and even whole cities in ruins. They showed ragged women cleaning rubble from the streets while the men sat, head in hands, on broken steps behind them. American GIs were shown passing out Hershey Chocolate bars to skinny, ragged children.

Other newsreels were much gloomier. Allied troops had discovered horrible conditions in prisoner-of-war camps, especially those housing Russian prisoners. And every week, it seemed, they found another of those horrible Death Camps. Some were as bad as Dachau, and some were even worse. And of course, the newsreels showed what was left of Germany—its cities in ruins, its armies broken, its people ragged and hungry. But after six years of war, and the discovery of the Death Camps, there was little sympathy for the Germans.

CHAPTER 29

June 1945

Spring ripened into summer, and still the war in the Pacific raged on. Almost daily, a convoy passed the Wests' house, heading for San Francisco. The trucks were mostly open now, so anyone could see what they carried. Nobody feared enemy spies anymore. War materials and new soldiers were all being sent to fight the Japanese. Casualties mounted as more and more American men hit the beaches of islands closer and closer to the Japanese homeland. In June, the Marines finally captured Okinawa. Now, nothing remained but Japan itself.

Saturday morning, June 9th, Elaine and all the kids in the neighborhood were playing baseball in the street. Since no one actually had a baseball, the "ball" was an empty evaporated milk can. Evaporated milk cans were used as substitute balls because, instead of being opened by a can opener, milk cans were punctured by an ice pick. Evaporated milk cans were also used to play "kick the can".

From her spot in right field, Elaine spotted Mother heading toward the victory garden with a basket. Knowing that nobody would likely miss her anyway, since she could not catch or throw well, Elaine peeled off from the game and ran to join Mother.

"May I help, Mother," she asked.

"Yes, of course, Elaine, you can dig carrots while I pick green beans. Oh, there's Gertrude." Mother walked over to where Mrs. Schultz had just come into the garden.

"Hello, Gertrude, how are you?"

"About as well as can be expected, Alice." Something in her voice seemed distant, desperate and sad.

Mother seemed puzzled by Mrs. Schultz's mood. Elaine kept digging carrots, but she was listening. She, too, was puzzled by the sadness and worry in Mrs. Schultz's voice.

165

"I haven't seen Fred. It must be wonderful having him home again after all this time. How is he?" Mother's voice was light and cheerful.

Elaine had tried to keep track of Fred throughout the war. She knew that he had led a platoon in the D-Day Invasion and then fought his way into Germany. He had served bravely and had been quickly promoted to captain. But then, suddenly, he had been discharged early from the Army. Kids at school said only the injured were being discharged. Elaine worried about him when she heard that. She thought he might have lost a leg, or worse. Neighbors were talking about him, but no one had seen him since he came home. As far as anyone knew, he never left the house.

"Oh, Alice," Mrs. Schultz seemed relieved to be able to confide in someone at last, "he's not at all well! Oh, there's no injury you can see, but he's just not himself. He doesn't do anything; maybe eat a little. Even then, he just picks at his food, and never looks up. He acts as if he's eating alone. The rest of the time, he stays in his room, sits on the bed, and stares at the wall or at some photos he brought home with him."

Mrs. Schultz pulled closer to Mother then, as if to tell her a secret. But Mrs. Schultz was half deaf, and always spoke a little louder than most people. Elaine had no trouble hearing her: "At night I hear him sometimes, walking in his room, just around and around. Once, I swear, I even heard him crying. We try to talk with him, but he doesn't seem to hear us—he just stares into the air, like so." And with that, Mrs. Schultz looked up into the sky, like she had spotted a plane. It was so convincing that Elaine turned around to look, just in case. But there was nothing there.

Mrs. Schultz continued: "He never talks. His eyes are always empty." The tears came to her eyes and she stammered, "It's like he's not our son anymore."

She stood back and stared at Mother awhile. Finally, she added: "We knew it was an invasion of his privacy, but Heinrich and I felt we had to know what was bothering him." Mrs. Schultz pulled in close again, "so one time, when he was in the bathroom, I slipped into his room and looked at those photos. They were horrible! They were scenes of one of those—eh—Nazi camps of death! And he was in some of the photos—our Freidrich!—standing beside heaps of dead bodies, and taking care of starving men, women, and even children. It must have been his command that liberated one of those camps. It has done something to his mind—seeing these things—and now he is so ill! We wonder if he will ever be the same!"

Mother gave her friend what hope and comfort she could. "It must have been extremely difficult having to make decisions about how best to help people who had suffered so much. I don't imagine deciding what to do with the guards who had managed the horror was easy either, and then having to govern the nearby civilians, who must have known what was going on. Nothing in his experience or studies of history could have prepared him for what he had to take charge of. It must have worn him out to the bottom of his soul.

"And to be from German parents!" Mother looked at Mrs. Schultz, "good, God-fearing German parents, who would never do such a thing. And yet here he was, in the country where you were born… I can't imagine what it must have done to him!"

Mrs. Schultz looked as though she was ready to burst into tears, and Elaine saw that Mother knew it. "But Gertrude, you know that there were men in the last war who saw as bad, and worse. They got better. It took time, but they are better now, and Freddy will be also. Prayer and time are great healers. With enough of both, he'll probably be all right."

Since Elaine was not included in the conversation, she pretended not to hear. The talk reminded her of the newsreel of Dachau. Seeing scenes of the camp in a movie theater had bothered her for days. It bothered her sometimes still—she found that she no longer had nightmares about polio, but she had one or two about those camps. What must it have been like to be there in person! How could human beings treat other humans with such cruelty? Is that what war was really about? And how could she—or Mother, or Father, or anyone for that matter—have prevented something like that from happening? Deep in thought, Elaine waited until Mother had gathered her vegetables and then rejoined the baseball game.

After months of hard fighting, General MacArthur announced the complete liberation of the Philippines on July 5th. Many people breathed a sigh of relief as they heard back from loved ones who had been imprisoned by the Japanese for three and a half years. Still others were informed that their loved ones had been murdered by the Japanese, or had died of disease in the camps.

Even now, though, some people still knew nothing. Mrs. Atkins, Elaine's fourth grade teacher, still heard no word from her husband. That Sunday, as they sat in church, Elaine looked across the aisle at Mrs. Atkins. She sat motionless through the whole sermon, her eyes fixed on the blue banner with its stars, silver and gold. 'But which is he?' Elaine could almost hear Mrs. Atkins' thoughts, and could feel her desperate longing—just to know, once and for all, what had happened to her husband.

And still, nearly every day, a long convoy of trucks would roll by the Wests' house.

Experienced, battle-hardened troops that were not needed for the European occupation were being made ready to go to the Pacific for the invasion of Japan. For some, this would be their fourth beach landing— after landing at North Africa, Italy, and France, they would now storm the shores of Japan. The whole country's attention shifted west. Troops coming home from Europe were given a short leave, and then reassigned to the Pacific. The number of truck convoys passing the Wests' house increased as more and more of the war materials and men were shifted to the War in the Pacific. When Elaine heard a convoy coming, she'd run outside and try to catch a glimpse of the soldiers' faces. They seemed so much older now than they had been just a year before—sad eyes and mouths set in solemn, grim, determined expressions. The radio blared endlessly about the upcoming invasion of Japan and the terrible bloodbath it would be. D-Day was still fresh in the minds of all Americans, and on the street, people now spoke of "X-Day".

CHAPTER 30

August, 1945

Before school started, the Wests were once again going on vacation. But they were not going to Santa Cruz this year. The tires on the car were too thin to be trusted for such a long trip. Instead they had rented a cabin at Shaver Lake, in the nearby mountains.

"I'm going to the store to get the food to take with us. Anybody want to come?" Mother called.

"I do." Elaine hopped up from the sofa where she had been reading a book. Any outing with Mother would break the monotony of the summer.

"Good," said Mother. "Anybody else?" When there was no answer, she said, "Then Sara, you look out for Billy. Billy, mind your sister."

"I will," said Sara.

"I will," echoed Billy.

As Mother and Elaine walked together down the street Elaine asked, "What are we going to do at Shaver Lake?"

"Oh, we'll swim and hike and read, and be sure and bring your Monopoly set and some other games to play." Mother replied.

They continued to talk, merrily, planning the vacation until they got to the store.

When they left the store, Mother had a shopping bag full of groceries and Elaine was licking a Popsicle she had bought with some of her rabbit money. Elaine was pleased that Mother had bought marshmallows to toast over a campfire, but disappointed that the butcher had no hot dogs to roast or bacon to go with their eggs in the morning. She was tired of the war and its shortages.

"When is this war going to end? It just keeps going on and on!" Elaine said.

"I don't know," sighed Mother. "Who knows how long the Japanese will fight after we invade. They know they're already beaten, but they just keep fighting anyway. It took almost a year after we invaded France before the Germans surrendered. Who knows how long it will take after we invade Japan."

"When are we going to invade? All we hear is talk, but it seems like the Army's taking a long time!"

"It will have to be soon. There doesn't seem to be anything else to do to end this war, and we can't give the Japanese time to rearm. But nobody will know the exact date until it happens. When we finally do invade, surprise will be about the only thing on our side."

They walked on in silence, Elaine still licking her Popsicle. She had to work at it quickly, before the heat melted the orange flavored ice off the stick.

"Oh! There's Gertrude," Mother said, as they stopped at the victory garden. She walked toward her friend, and Elaine tagged along.

"Hello Gertrude. How are you?"

"All is very good! My Friedrich is finally come home, and he is well in mind and body!"

"What happened? What made the change?"

"I do not know this," said Mrs. Schultz. "It is time maybe, or prayer. Anyway, the day before yesterday, my Friedrich, he left his room, took those horrible photos out to the barrel in the back yard and burned them. Then he comes into the kitchen and says, 'Mother, would you fix me a sandwich, please? I'm suddenly very hungry.' I could hardly see to spread the mayonnaise on the bread; mine eyes were so full of tears!" Mrs. Schultz was visibly different—straighter, more composed.

"Since then, all we do is talk, my Friedrich and I. He wanted to know about how it has been at home, this past year. He wanted to know if the school is hiring again. It's so wonderful to have him truly home at last! He says he's anxious to get back in the classroom, teaching American history again. He is down at the School Administration Building now, to see about getting his job back at the high school in time to start the school year."

Mother responded with joy in her voice. "Oh, I'm so pleased I'm sure the high school will be pleased to have him back. He was such a good teacher. And I wouldn't worry about his job—I hear a lot of teachers are anxious to quit or retire as soon as the men come back to replace them."

Mother interrupted her conversation long enough to say, "Elaine, when you finish your Popsicle, pick the tomatoes that are ripe. Get some that are not too ripe also, and we'll take them with us tomorrow." Then she went back to talking with Mrs. Schultz. Elaine busied herself in the garden, happy that things were well with Freddy again.

CHAPTER 31

August 4, 1945

Early the next morning, the Wests left for a two-week vacation. The road to Shaver Lake was very steep and winding. Because the trip was only two hours long, Elaine was allowed a window seat and Billy had to sit in the middle. Sometimes, if Elaine looked out the window, she could see the highway they had already traveled on almost directly beneath her. It made her stomach feel sick. "I feel like I might throw up!" she wailed.

"Keep your eyes on the road ahead. Don't look over the edge, and you'll feel better," said Mother. They kept going up, and up, and up.

Halfway up the grade, they stopped at a turn out. Everybody got out and stretched their legs. Father took off the radiator's cap and everyone watched while the remaining water turned to steam and hissed into the air. Father filled the radiator with water from a small brook beside the road. Before they had all gotten back into the car another car pulled in. Steam was coming from its hood as the driver got out to get water. It took another hour of winding up the steep grade before they got to Shaver Lake.

Elaine had seen Shaver Lake before, but had forgotten how beautiful it was—a shimmering, glassy sheet of crystal blue water surrounded by mountains covered with pine forests on three sides. The fourth side was composed of the huge concrete dam that had turned a small valley into a lake. They drove past the dam and past a group of small businesses, past the Shaver Lake Lodge and into the forest. About a mile farther along they turned off onto a dirt road and pulled in beside a small cabin.

The children rushed inside so that they could change into their bathing suits and make it out to the lake while there was still plenty of light. The cabin was supplied with a two-burner propane stove, a sink with running cold water, a tiny counter a table, and six chairs in the main room. In one bedroom there was a double bed. Upstairs, under the steep roof, there were six cots. There was a large porch with lawn chairs and a picnic table. After lunch they unpacked the car then hurried to the lake for a quick swim. The water was cold, even though it had sat in the sun all summer long. The large rocks beside the lake were warm from the sun and perfect for sunbathing.

While the rest of the family swam, Father dug a pit near the cabin and lined it with rocks. He then put a gunnysack over the rocks and put the milk, eggs, and fresh fruit and vegetables into the pit. He covered the food with another gunnysack and poured lake water over it to keep it cool, just like he'd done with the watermelons and the rabbit hutches.

Before the rest of the family was out of bed Monday morning, Father took the car and drove to one of the many trout streams that fed the lake. He hoped to catch fish for their dinner. The rest of the family spent the mornings hiking and gathering firewood. Since they were on National Forest land, it was legal to collect any piece of wood that was dead and down. There was not much firewood left since it was the end of the summer, so they had to go quite a distance before they found as much wood as they could carry back. Most of what they gathered to burn were pinecones. Lots of sugar pines grew around the lake. Their cones were huge, sometimes as long as fifteen to eighteen inches. They saved some of the larger, unbroken cones to decorate the fireplace at home, and set the rest by the firepit to burn later.

After a lunch of sandwiches, they hiked down to the beach to swim. On the bank of the lake there was a huge, smooth boulder. Part of the boulder had a gentle slope that made it easy to climb. Another part stuck out into the lake and had a steep slope. The girls quickly figured out that the boulder made a terrific water-slide. They had a great time sliding and splashing into the lake. They played at the lake until a wind came up and they began to get cold.

When they got back to the cabin, Father was napping. In a bucket near the table were several good-sized trout. War had improved the fishing, because so many fishermen were now overseas. The children changed clothes and found it was still pleasant to play outside once they were dry. That evening, Father roasted the fish on a rack over the coals of a campfire, while Mother cooked green beans and potatoes on the stove in the cabin. They ate on the porch of the cabin, enjoying the still evening air, and the beauty of a sunset over the lake. After they washed the dinner dishes, the girls stirred up the coals in the fire pit and toasted marshmallows until dark.

The next morning—Tuesday—Father again went fishing while the rest of the family just stayed around the cabin. It was so relaxed and peaceful with no radio and few other people. That afternoon they again went to the lake. This time Sara brought the soap along. Soaping the boulder made it really slick and increased the speed of the slide. They had even more fun than they had had the day before, as Mother sat and read under a nearby tree. When the time came, all four of them were reluctant to leave.

Father returned to the cabin early. He had caught his daily limit of fish. He was in a good mood and suggested that they drive down to the lodge for ice cream cones.

As soon as she saw the crowd outside the lodge, Elaine knew something important had happened. There were no parking places left near the lodge, so they had to park quite a distance away and walk. As they approached the cabin, they saw that a huge crowd gathered. People spilled out of the door and stood in small clusters in front of the building, speaking excitedly to one another.

As they drew closer to the crowd, Elaine heard someone say, "One bomb!"

"A whole city!" said a woman.

"Are you sure it's true?" said a man.

"When?" asked another voice.

"One bomb!" said still another voice

"A large city?"

"Bigger than Fresno?"

As they made their way through the crowd the same phrases were spoken over and over again by different people. Elaine struggled to make sense of it. It was nearly half an hour before she finally gathered the whole story. Apparently, a terrible new bomb had been dropped on a Japanese military base in a Japanese city with a name that no one could pronounce. The city was in ruins and thousands were dead, all from a single bomb. Elaine tried to imagine it, but couldn't. Everyone was talking about the bomb, but it seemed like pure fantasy. It was difficult to get any real facts.

In the morning, instead of going fishing, Father hurried to the lodge to buy a newspaper. He found, though, that the newspaper was a day old and had no news of the bomb. He tried again the next day but the paper was sold out before he got there. Still, a copy of the front page was tacked up on the wall. When he returned he was almost giddy—Elaine couldn't remember ever seeing him like that before. "It's true!" he said, "about the bomb—President Truman made the announcement yesterday—it's hard to believe, but—well, there's a copy of the announcement on the cabin door. Come on, I'll show you!"

They all got into the car and drove to the lodge. There, Mother read out loud the announcement President Truman had made to the nation:

"Sixteen hours ago, an American airplane dropped one bomb on Hiroshima, an important Japanese Army base. The bomb had more power than 20,000 tons of T.N.T. It had more than two thousand times the power of the British 'Grand Slam' which is the largest bomb ever yet used in the history of warfare…

"It is an atomic bomb. It is a harnessing of the basic power of the universe. The force from which the sun draws its power has been loosed against those who brought war to the Far East…"

"Maybe now," Mother sighed, "the Japanese will surrender."

They all went back to the cabin. Elaine wasn't sure how to feel. All she could think of were the faces of the soldiers she'd seen in the convoys—stony, sad eyes set in grim, gritty faces.

After lunch, Mother and the children again went swimming. When they got back from the lake Father was gone. He left a note: "Gone fishing. Back at dusk."

He came back with fish in time for a late dinner. The next morning—

Friday—Father went fishing again. When he came back they hurried to the lodge and learned that another huge bomb had been dropped on another Japanese target. But still, there was no word of Japanese surrender.

That Sunday, the little church at Shaver Lake was packed. People were even standing outside. Everyone prayed for a Japanese surrender and an end to the bloodshed.

It was next Wednesday—August 15, 1945—that the news finally came. Japan had surrendered. The atomic bomb had killed thousands of Japanese, but had saved the lives of millions more, since no Japanese soldiers or civilians would die defending the Japanese home islands.

For America, the ordeal was over. There was a shared feeling of relief. There would be no invasion. Thousands of American boys who would have died in the invasion would now come home. Everyone celebrated! Every car that came up the hill honked its horn over and over. Elaine could hear each car, first at a faint distance, then louder and louder as it got closer and closer. Some cars stopped at the lodge, but others continued up the hill, passing their cabin and then moving on to become fainter and fainter as they retreated into the distance. There was dancing in the lodge each evening but children weren't allowed inside because the lodge served alcohol at the dance. The Wests celebrated at their campfire by popping popcorn and toasting marshmallows over the coals.

Sunday morning, they went to church to join others in thanking God for an end to the war. They didn't swim after lunch. They couldn't. They had worn holes into the bottom of their swimsuits by sliding down the bolder into the lake. "That's okay," Mother said cheerily, "we'll be able to buy new suits for all of us soon enough!"

That Sunday evening, Father drove the family down from the mountains. It was dusk when they came around the corner and viewed Fresno below them. Elaine gasped. The city lights were on! Billboards, streetlights, shop lights, theater lights, and neon signs. Lights were everywhere! Although the need for darkness had lessened over the years, the lights had remained off as a symbol of the war. Now, the city was celebrating with light.

"Let's drive downtown," suggested Mother.

"Oh yes! Let's!" chorused the kids from the back seat.

It was just like before the war. They drove downtown just to see the lights. Lots of people were downtown. The war had ended four days ago, but the celebration was still going on. Cars roared up and down the main street with people shouting out the windows and honking their horns.

"Honk the horn, Daddy. Honk the horn!" the kids chorused from the back seat. All the cars were honking. There were noisy crowds on every street corner. Sidewalks were crowded with civilians and airmen alike. People were overjoyed that the war was over, and the long-dreaded invasion of Japan would never happen. Elaine was delighted to see that the fox was once again running up, never down, the sign in front of the fur store. Billy recognized the truck, fire engine, and car running across the front of the toy store. Everyone enjoyed the brightly lit windows, the streetlights and the crowds.

When the Wests got home, Elaine saw that the tower on the Tower Theater was once again shining out over the roofs of the neighboring houses. An old friend had returned.

Like everyone else, the Wests set aside time to go to the movies that week, just to see the newsreel. There, on the screen, they saw the mushroom cloud that had changed the world forever. The picture had been taken in New Mexico in July, when the atomic bomb had first been tested. A scientist explained how the bomb worked. There were no pictures of Hiroshima and Nagasaki, the two Japanese cities. They could not be taken until the formal surrender took place and Allied troops landed in Japan.

What impressed Elaine the most from the newsreel was not the mushroom cloud. It was the pictures of battle-weary marines sitting on an island in the Pacific, with tears of joy and relief streaming down their faces. Those men knew that they now had a future. They would not be cut to ribbons on the beach by Japanese machineguns. They would indeed be home alive, if not in '45 than surely in early '46.

CHAPTER 32

October, 1945

Elaine went back to school just a few weeks after the family returned from Shaver Lake. Her sixth grade classroom was in the school's auditorium, and it was full almost to bursting. Countless men had come through California in the last four months, and in some cases, their families had moved with them. But moving, adjusting, crowding into smaller rooms with more people—all these things seemed easier, somehow. It was as if the whole world were being tossed about on the wind, dancing like a feather.

American servicemen started coming home almost immediately, but there were still thousands overseas, waiting to return. Mother explained that it would take a long time to move that many men. For months, every ship that sailed from the old world to the new had been full of returning servicemen. But not all of the men were coming home. Some were needed in Europe and Japan as part of the military occupation and cleanup.

One of the ships sent to bring the men back from the War in the Pacific took Rae Dean and her mother to Honolulu to join Rae Dean's father. Elaine feared she might never see Rae Dean again, but clung to Rae Dean's promise that she would come back to visit.

Veterans returning to Fresno went looking for work. Grandpa, like many other older workers, was happy to turn his job over to a veteran and retire. But there were few new jobs to be had. All the factories had been tooled to make weapons, and now they were shut down and re-tooling for civilian things—things like cars and shoes and toys. So most of the men who came home just loafed around, or went fishing, or played baseball, or just enjoyed being home while they waited for the economy to change over to peacetime. Thousands of veterans were planning to take advantage of the government's offer to pay their college expenses, and were preparing to go to college when the next term began.

News continued to pour out of Germany and Japan about all the terrible things the Germans and Japanese had done during the war. There was outrage unlike any the world had ever known. The radio was full of talk of punishing the people responsible for the Death Camps, the torture of civilians and prisoners, and other terrible acts. But nobody seemed to agree on how to punish such unspeakable crimes. The atrocities were so beyond belief that they somehow seemed beyond justice as well.

Rationing continued. Food, especially meat, was still in short supply. Mother explained: "The New World is now feeding the Old. In much of Europe and Asia, the farms had been the battlegrounds. Many fields are nothing now but mud and weeds. As for meat, soldiers from both sides have killed and eaten all the livestock, down to the last goat or chicken."

The Japanese in America, now called Japanese-Americans because of the bravery of their sons, were released from the camps and given transportation home. They returned to find their businesses gone, other people living in their houses and farming their land. There was no payment for their loss and no apology for their imprisonment. They were just shipped back and dropped off in the towns they had come from over three years before.

At the same time that the Japanese-Americans were trying to rebuild their lives, the newsreels were showing the heroic actions of their sons. The 442nd Regimental Combat Team and the 100th Infantry Battalion, both made up entirely of Japanese-Americans, were among the most decorated units in the war. Many of these same Japanese-Americans, whose parents had lived in camps surrounded by barbed wire for almost four years, were now being sent to Japan to help with the occupation. Their knowledge of the Japanese language and culture would be a great help in remaking Japan.

Miko's family never returned to Fresno, or if they did, they didn't visit Grandpa. Elaine wondered if anyone would plant strawberries again. Strawberries had not been in the stores since the Japanese had been taken.

Just before school started that September, Mother came to Elaine after church. "Elaine, I thought you should know," Mother said.

"Know what?"

"You remember Mrs. Atkins, your fourth grade teacher? Well, her husband—Captain Atkins—he's been reclassified as KIA—Killed in Action."

Elaine was crushed. Mother told her the full story.

Captain Atkins had survived the Japanese invasion of the Philippines. He had been taken prisoner, and survived almost four years under horrible conditions in a Japanese Prisoner of War camp. In early 1945, in order to keep the surviving American prisoners from being liberated by advancing American forces, the Japanese had started shipping them to Japan. Conditions on the prison ships were so bad that the survivors would later call them the "hell ships". Captain Atkins had been among one of the first groups sent on one of these "hell ships".

Ships carrying prisoners were supposed to be marked with a white cross, so that they would not be targeted by enemy planes and submarines. But the Japanese ship on which Captain Atkins was being transported had been unmarked. American bombers on patrol had mistaken it for part of a Japanese troop convoy and attacked it. The Japanese crew simply abandoned the ship, and it was destroyed. Captain Atkins—along with five hundred other American servicemen—had survived over three years of horror only to be killed by his own countrymen.

Elaine didn't know what to make of it. But she knew that Mrs. Atkins would be devastated. She wished that there was something she could do, but felt completely powerless. After the newsreels of D-Day, of Dachau and of Bataan, and the stories leaking out of Japan about the atomic bombings there, Elaine was almost numb to it all.

The next morning, Elaine went to school and squeezed into her desk at the back of the school auditorium. She knew how the day would begin. But she had little idea how that day would change her; how it would leave her with a memory that would haunt her forever afterward.

"Students," announced Miss Worth from her desk on the corner of the stage of the old auditorium, "today we have a special treat. Arthur Lea is going to tell us about what it was like living in the Philippines..."

CHAPTER 33

The Pledge

Back in the sixth grade classroom at John Muir Elementary School, Arthur had finally stopped sobbing. But Elaine was still thinking of the war. All through the war, there had been talk of things getting back to normal, but the atomic bomb had changed all that. The atomic bomb was the only kind of bomb anyone talked about anymore. In fact, everyone called it "The Bomb", as if all other kinds of bombs no longer existed. It was clear that The Bomb had changed the world forever. People were determined that the future not be like the past. There could never be another war. If there were ever a World War III, the human race could be destroyed by this terrible new weapon. Exactly how to make The Bomb was America's secret for now, but everyone knew that in time other countries would learn. Everyone knew now that if mankind itself were to survive, the nations of the world would have to learn to live together without war. Mother had said, "Nations are made up of people. People must learn to live in peace. We can all help by living peacefully with our neighbors."

Elaine looked over at Arthur. He was still wiping his eyes, and every once in a while he would let out slight sob. Elaine felt water welling up in her eyes also. She closed them to stop the tears, and made a silent pledge to do her share for peace.

THE END